THE PARADOX OF INESCAPABLE OWNERSHIP

DEEPAK RAJANINATH MOKASHI

notionpress.com

INDIA • SINGAPORE • MALAYSIA

Copyright © Deepak Rajaninath Mokashi 2025
All Rights Reserved.

ISBN
Hardcase 979-8-89984-235-1
Paperback 979-8-89929-705-2

This book has been published with all efforts taken to make the material error-free after the consent of the author. However, the author and the publisher do not assume and hereby disclaim any liability to any party for any loss, damage, or disruption caused by errors or omissions, whether such errors or omissions result from negligence, accident, or any other cause.

While every effort has been made to avoid any mistake or omission, this publication is being sold on the condition and understanding that neither the author nor the publishers or printers would be liable in any manner to any person by reason of any mistake or omission in this publication or for any action taken or omitted to be taken or advice rendered or accepted on the basis of this work. For any defect in printing or binding the publishers will be liable only to replace the defective copy by another copy of this work then available.

Contents

Preface

The Paradox of Inescapable Ownership is a natural continuation of my earlier work, an exploration of corporate strategy and leadership through the lens of ethics. It stands as a manifesto for modern leaders navigating complexity, ambiguity, and moral nuance, urging them to confront the contradictions of responsibility and ownership with courage, clarity, and compassion.

At the heart of this work lies a simple but inescapable truth:

"You may avoid responsibility. But responsibility won't avoid you."

Building on this premise, the book offers a bold and penetrating exploration of one of leadership's most misunderstood dynamics: responsibility. It challenges the prevailing notion that responsibility is a choice, presenting a blend of philosophical inquiry and practical guidance for leaders grappling with complexity, moral ambiguity, and invisible influence.

Structured across thirteen original chapters and a compelling case study, the book reveals an uncomfortable paradox: even silence, inaction, and avoidance generate their own form of ownership. Whether in the context of institutions, teams, or systems, the unseen weight of decisions, those deferred, denied, or inherited, continues to shape cultures, relationships, and futures.

Covering themes such as invisible decisions, over-responsibility traps, emotional burdens, and legacy leadership, the book introduces frameworks including the *Ownership Discernment Matrix, the Ownership Compass,* and the integrative *Ownership Mandal.* These tools enable leaders to identify their true sphere of influence across four realms: *Self, Others, Systems, and Legacy,* while nurturing a conscious leadership cycle: *Awareness, Action, Aftermath.*

Blending philosophical depth with organisational insight, *The Paradox of Inescapable Ownership* is not a manual of directives; it is an invitation to pause, to reflect, and to approach leadership as stewardship rather than control.

Insight

The journey begins not in the midst of crisis, but at a deeper threshold where leaders begin to question not their capability, but the very nature of what they are truly responsible for. The book walks readers through paradoxes rather than toward quick fixes, helping them discern what must be held and what must be released with grace, courage, and clarity.

CHAPTER 1

The Inescapable Ownership Paradox

Leadership often comes with the illusion of choice regarding responsibility. Many believe they can delegate, defer, or even deny responsibility, but paradoxically, these very actions create their own forms of ownership. Whether acknowledged or not, responsibility is inescapable because every decision, or lack thereof, has a consequence. Leaders must recognise that failing to act is itself an action, one with repercussions that they cannot evade. The key is not in deciding whether to take ownership, but in understanding how that ownership manifests. Leaders who embrace this paradox operate with greater awareness, shaping their legacy intentionally rather than by accident.

1.1 What if Refusing Responsibility Still Makes You Responsible?

You don't always choose ownership; sometimes, it chooses you.

We live in a world where disclaiming responsibility has become a craft. Layers of bureaucracy, cleverly worded disclaimers, and well-structured silos allow individuals and institutions to distance themselves from consequences. And yet, paradoxically, even in our attempts to sidestep ownership, responsibility often boomerangs back, inescapable, invisible, and ultimately unavoidable.

Let us pose a troubling question: *What if refusing responsibility still makes you responsible?*

This question is not rhetorical. It is foundational.

In a ship at sea, if the navigator falls asleep at the wheel, the ocean doesn't excuse the vessel. The storm doesn't pause. The crew doesn't become magically immune to danger. Whether the navigator claims responsibility or not, the outcome of their inaction remains firmly theirs. Ownership, in such contexts, is not contractual; it is natural. It flows not from willingness but from position, from context, from consequence.

This is the paradox: Responsibility is not always assumed; sometimes, it is simply conferred. By role, by circumstance, by the ripples one creates or fails to contain.

In leadership, especially, abdication is a myth. Silence is a statement. Inaction is a choice. And the refusal to act, ironically, often constitutes the most defining form of action. The paradox is that we are bound to outcomes even when we claim detachment from inputs. If one chooses to look away while harm is occurring, the moral and systemic consequences don't look away in return. You are involved, whether you raise your hand or keep it tucked in your pocket.

This understanding demolishes the comforting illusion of neutrality. One cannot escape accountability merely by declining to engage. The leader who refuses to make a hard call is still responsible for the vacuum they leave behind. The individual who stands by as systems falter becomes, in time, part of the system's failure.

Refusing responsibility, then, is not an escape route; it is a route of delayed reckoning.

History, too, bears this out. The passive witness, the indifferent bystander, the bureaucrat who followed orders without question; all found, eventually, that they were held to account, not just by courts, but by conscience and consequence. Absence of action does not imply absence of effect.

We are each a node in a vast web of interdependence. Every choice, including the choice to not act, sends out vibrations. The paradox of inescapable ownership is not a philosophical musing; it is a lived reality, especially for those entrusted with power, influence, or even knowledge.

And so, *a fundamental truth emerges:* Responsibility does not wait for your consent. It arrives uninvited, anchored to your influence and your place in the unfolding of events.

To refuse it is only to misunderstand its nature.

1.1.1   The Shadow Ownership Model

To comprehend the inescapable nature of responsibility, imagine a framework I call the Shadow Ownership Model. This model distinguishes between Declared Responsibility and Shadow Responsibility; one visible, the other hidden but equally potent.

1. Declared Responsibility

This is the responsibility one acknowledges, accepts, or is officially assigned. It includes roles, duties, and accountabilities that are contractually or culturally recognised. Think of job titles, delegations, or task lists. This is the visible ownership; the front stage of action.

2. Shadow Responsibility

This is the responsibility one cannot escape, even when unacknowledged. It arises from:

Influence held but not exercised
Power known but not used
Knowledge possessed but withheld

Position occupied during a critical moment
Inaction in the face of clear stakes

Shadow Responsibility is the backstage of ownership. It often remains unspoken; but never without consequence. It exists in the gaps, the silences, and the moral corners leaders try to avoid. It is invisible at first, but becomes visible when impact unfurls.

3. The Paradox Unveiled

Most people operate under the illusion that by not stepping forward, they can step away. But the Shadow Ownership Model reveals the flaw in that logic. Even without active engagement, your latent power binds you to outcomes. You may not accept the role, but the system, the circumstance, and the consequences still assign it to you.

Just as a shadow follows the body, responsibility follows relevance. Where you could have made a difference, your non-action becomes a silent decision; just as decisive, just as binding.

The Shadow Ownership Model	
Responsibility has two faces: **one seen, one hidden – but both binding**	
Declared Responsibility **(Visible)**	**Shadow Responsibility** **(Invisible)**
Acknowledged and Accepted Form: Job titles, task lists, formal roles Positions Front Stage Assigned Project Manager Elected Leader Formal Decision-Maker	Unacknowledged, but Unavoidable Power unused, knowledge withheld Examples: Staying silent despite knowing the truth, Holding a key position during the crisis, Being an observer

The Paradox Unveiled	
Responsibility does not wait for your consent. It rises from your relevance.	
Myth	**Reality**
If I don't act, I am not responsible. No one asked me, so I am not accountable.	Your action is action with consequences. Your position already made you part of the outcome the moment it was assigned.
Analogy: Body and Shadow	
The Body	**The Shadow**
Declared Responsibility	Shadow Responsibility.

1.1.2   Case Study: The Silent Compliance Officer – A Lesson from a Major Banking Crisis

In the late 2010s, a major Indian public sector bank faced a high-profile crisis involving fraudulent Letters of Undertaking (LoUs) issued without proper authorisation. While the fraud itself was orchestrated by a few key players, what emerged in the aftermath was equally telling; the role of those who could have acted, but didn't.

Among them was the Chief Compliance Officer; a person who, while not directly involved in issuing the LoUs, had access to systems, red flags, and reports that indicated irregularities. However, the officer neither escalated the anomalies nor took corrective action, believing it was 'not in my job description' to intervene unless formally instructed.

On paper, the officer had no declared responsibility in that transactional chain.

But in retrospect, when the scam was exposed, regulatory bodies, internal investigators, and public opinion turned toward those who held latent influence; who sat at critical junctions of information and oversight but chose not to act. The compliance officer became a textbook case of Shadow Responsibility, where responsibility was denied but the consequences still arrived.

The paradox came alive:

By not taking responsibility, the officer didn't escape it; he embodied it.

He lost his position, his reputation was damaged, and even though he wasn't a perpetrator, the public and internal stakeholders saw him as complicit by silence.

Why This Illustrates the Paradox

Position granted him influence, even if not formal authority over the fraud.

Inaction became interpreted as consent or dereliction, not neutrality.

Ownership was not given by designation but by the consequence of the outcome.

This case brings the Shadow Ownership Model into sharp focus. In complex systems, especially corporate hierarchies, those who occupy critical observation posts are as accountable for what they ignore as they are for what they do.

1.2   How Inaction, Avoidance, or Delegation Still Create Ownership; Whether Acknowledged or Not

Responsibility does not dissipate in the absence of action. It lingers, often unnoticed, like a shadow cast by decision; even when the decision is to do nothing. *The paradox is this:* even when we stay silent, we are speaking; even when we do nothing, we are acting. In leadership, responsibility is not just about stepping forward, but also about understanding the consequences of holding back.

1.2.1 The Fallacy of Avoidance

Leaders often fall prey to the illusion that avoidance is neutral. That by not choosing, not intervening, or not engaging, they remain untouched by the consequences of a situation. But reality refuses to cooperate with this illusion. Systems respond not just to what leaders do, but also to what they choose not to do.

Avoidance is not absence of ownership; it is a silent acceptance of a different kind of authorship; one without deliberate voice, but with real-world consequences. When a leader refrains from addressing toxicity in a team, sidesteps conflict, or ignores ethical compromise, they are not distancing themselves from responsibility. They are embedding themselves deeper into it. They are co-authoring outcomes through omission.

1.2.2 Delegation Is Not Abdication

Delegation is a vital tool in any leader's arsenal. But delegation without oversight is abdication in disguise. When leaders hand over responsibility without clarity, alignment, or accountability, they are not shedding ownership; they are merely shifting the mechanics of execution while retaining the ethical and strategic burden.

The paradox here is sharp: the more you delegate without understanding, the more your ownership of the consequences grows. The chain of accountability never truly breaks. Even when the action originates from others, the source of the environment, the system, or the enabling conditions often points back to the leader.

A ship captain may not be in the engine room, but if the engine fails due to poor maintenance protocols approved under their command, they still bear the consequences. Delegation, therefore, demands stewardship, not distance.

1.2.3   Inaction as a Strategic Act

In some situations, inaction can be a deliberate strategy. Waiting, observing, or choosing not to intervene immediately may be wise. But even then, inaction is not a vacuum; it is a choice. And like every choice, it carries the weight of consequence. The problem arises not with inaction itself, but with the failure to own it.

Many leaders hide behind the cloak of passivity, hoping that time, systems, or people will resolve the issue. When that fails, the fallout still lands at their doorstep. Ownership doesn't require your permission to manifest. It emerges from the reality of influence and role, not from intention or declaration.

1.2.4   The Hidden Cost of Non-Decision

Non-decision is not neutrality; it is a deferred burden. It places strain on those below, confusion among stakeholders, and often leads to suboptimal outcomes. The longer the delay in owning the problem, the more complex and compounded it becomes.

Ironically, in trying to avoid accountability through inaction or delay, one ends up owning not just the original issue, but also the ripple effects of failing to act. Inaction is not a shield; it is a silent builder of consequences.

Ownership, then, is not determined by preference. It is determined by position, influence, and the unavoidable interplay of choice and consequence. Whether one acts, avoids, or delegates; responsibility finds its way home.

In this paradox lies a profound leadership truth: You may choose not to decide, but you cannot escape what your indecision causes.

Let us now explore how this inescapable ownership manifests in different leadership settings - personal, professional, and institutional - and what it means to acknowledge the invisible lines that connect decisions, actions, and the self.

1.2.5 Case Study: The NBFC Liquidity Crisis – An Anatomy of Deferred Ownership

Consider the now well-known case of Infrastructure Leasing & Financial Services (IL&FS), an Indian infrastructure financing giant whose default in 2018 sent shockwaves through the country's financial ecosystem. The surface-level narrative was about bad loans and poor asset-liability management. But at the heart of it was a deeper story, one of delayed decisions, fragmented ownership, and chronic avoidance.

For years, red flags were raised; internal reports warned of unsustainable debt levels, skewed project returns, and opaque governance. However, no decisive action followed. Leadership tiers chose inaction in the name of optimism or institutional inertia. Regulatory bodies hesitated, citing jurisdictional boundaries. Promoters and board members allowed delegation to become dissociation.

When IL&FS finally defaulted, the consequence wasn't contained to the company. It triggered a liquidity crisis across the entire NBFC sector, choked credit to the real economy, and forced urgent systemic reforms. The irony? No single decision-maker had 'acted' irresponsibly in the traditional sense. But through non-action, avoidance, and abdication camouflaged as delegation, multiple entities shared inescapable ownership of the eventual collapse.

The lesson here is clear. When everyone assumes someone else will act, no one does, and the cost of that collective inaction can be profound. In the end, responsibility was distributed not by control, but by consequence.

Ownership, then, is not determined by preference. It is determined by position, influence, and the unavoidable interplay of choice and consequence. Whether one acts, avoids, or delegates; responsibility finds its way home.

In this paradox lies a profound leadership truth: You may choose not to decide, but you cannot escape what your indecision causes.

1.2.6   Mahabharat: Bhishm's Vow and the Weight of Inaction

The Mahabharat does not shy away from illustrating the burden of unacknowledged ownership. Among its many complex characters, Bhishm Pitamaha stands out as a towering figure of virtue, wisdom, and sacrifice. And yet, his silence in critical moments casts a long shadow over his legacy.

Bound by his vow of loyalty to the throne of Hastinapur, Bhishm watched as the court descended into moral decay. He witnessed Draupadi's humiliation in the Kuru court, a moment where dharm was not just tested; it was shattered. As the grand elder, revered by all and capable of commanding silence in a hall of chaos, he chose restraint over intervention. He rationalised his inaction through his vow, his role, and the constraints of royal protocol.

But history, and dharm, does not excuse inaction simply because it is well-intended or cleverly justified. Bhishm did not act, but he still owned the consequence. The disrobing of Draupadi marked a moral collapse, ignited a chain of vengeance, and became a defining trigger for the Kurukshetra war.

His later anguish, lying on the bed of arrows, was not merely from physical wounds. It was the burden of what he had failed to prevent, even though he had the power and stature to do so. In this light, Bhishm represents a profound truth: delegation to destiny does not absolve one from accountability, and avoidance cloaked in allegiance still generates ownership.

Just like in the IL&FS crisis, no single action sealed the fate of the kingdom. It was a series of silences, of good men doing nothing at the right time that allowed Adharm to flourish.

Both in epic and enterprise, the principle holds true:

'यद् भावि, तद् भवति' (What must happen will happen) is not a justification for passivity. It is a challenge to act wisely, because even destiny takes shape through our inaction.

Thus, whether in the corridors of ancient palaces or corporate boardrooms, the lesson remains: To avoid acting when one can, is not to escape responsibility; it is to silently endorse the consequences.

Leadership is not only measured by the decisions you make, but by the moments you chose silence when your voice could have changed the outcome.

Let us now explore how this inescapable ownership manifests in different leadership settings - personal, professional, and institutional - and what it means to acknowledge the invisible lines that connect decisions, actions, and the self.

1.3 Leadership isn't About Deciding If You're Responsible, But How You Manifest It

If the previous reflection established that ownership is inescapable, regardless of action, inaction, or delegation, then the true essence of leadership lies not in evading or accepting responsibility, but in consciously manifesting it.

Leadership does not grant us the luxury of neutrality. There is no meaningful leadership without responsibility, and there is no responsibility without consequence. The question is never, "Am I responsible?" - that has already been answered by your position, your influence, or even your silence. The real question is, "How do I choose to carry the weight I inevitably bear?"

1.3.1   The Myth of Conditional Responsibility

One of the most persistent myths in organisational life is that responsibility is a binary choice - that you are either in charge or you're not; that you either own the outcome or you don't. But leadership operates in a more complex, interwoven reality. Influence itself creates responsibility. The mere presence of leadership authority, even latent or symbolic, implies a duty to shape, guide, and respond.

This myth gives rise to leaders who act only when mandated, speak only when questioned, or own only when success arrives. But ownership is not a robe we wear in glory and discard in failure. It is a mantle that clings to us, regardless of whether we act heroically or hide in the wings.

1.3.2   Manifestation over Justification

Leaders often fall into the trap of justifying their roles, attempting to calibrate the scope of their responsibility by citing hierarchy, mandate, or domain. But this misses the point. In a world of inevitable ownership, leadership is not exercised through justification, but through manifestation, through what we do with the power we hold, whether large or small.

Do you intervene when others are demoralised? Do you take responsibility for a failure even if no one is blaming you? Do you speak the difficult truth, even when silence is safer?

These are the real tests. Leadership is not proven in times of clarity and celebration; it is revealed in moments of ambiguity, adversity, and moral crossroads. Manifesting responsibility means leaning in when it would be easier to lean away. It means claiming the unclaimed space where everyone is waiting for someone else to step forward.

1.3.3   The Ripple Effect of Ownership

When leaders manifest responsibility visibly and consistently, it creates a ripple effect: an ownership culture. People begin to take initiative not because it is assigned to them, but because they see it modelled. They begin to believe that owning a problem, even one they didn't cause, is not only acceptable, but honourable.

On the contrary, when leaders abdicate visible responsibility, either through silence, indifference, or excessive delegation, it generates uncertainty, blame, and inertia. Even competent teams flounder in the absence of manifested ownership. They are not waiting for orders; they are waiting for a signal that someone is truly present and accountable.

1.3.4   From Burden to Opportunity

Manifested responsibility is not just a burden; it is an opportunity. When leaders manifest their ownership boldly, it becomes a source of identity and integrity. It clarifies purpose. It earns trust. It transforms leadership from a title into a presence that others feel, even in your absence.

You may not always have control, but you always have ownership. And in the paradoxical architecture of leadership, this inescapable ownership does not confine you; it empowers you. You cannot choose whether you are responsible. But you can, and must, choose how that responsibility lives in your words, your actions, and your legacy.

1.4   How Leaders Can Consciously Manifest Ownership in Their Daily Behaviour

If leadership is less about the decision to be responsible and more about the manifestation of that responsibility, then it follows that true leaders must cultivate daily rituals of ownership. These aren't grand gestures; they're quiet, deliberate actions that communicate: *I am accountable. I am present. I care enough to act.*

Ownership is not a proclamation; it's a posture. And like all postures, it is developed through repetition, awareness, and intent.

1.4.1   Show Up Before You're Asked

Conscious ownership begins with proactive presence. Leaders who wait for permission to engage, or only surface during crises, unconsciously signal detachment. By contrast, leaders who show up before their name is called, whether in meetings, reviews, or informal conversations, demonstrate a readiness to own outcomes from the start.

A simple habit: Don't wait to be summoned; initiate. This applies not only to problems but to opportunities. When something good is emerging, own it and nurture it.

1.4.2   Finish Conversations Others Leave Halfway

Many issues in teams and organisations fester not because no one noticed, but because no one closed the loop. Leaders who practice daily ownership don't leave ambiguity hanging. They tie threads, clarify expectations, and address unresolved tensions, even when it's uncomfortable.

A practical ritual: End every key interaction with clarity: *What next? Who owns it? By when?*

1.4.3   Own the Unowned

In any system, there are 'orphaned' tasks, problems, or decisions: areas where no one feels directly accountable. Leaders who manifest ownership don't always wait for alignment. They step in, bridge gaps, and create momentum; then bring others along. They know that taking early ownership invites followership, not resentment.

A mindset shift: The more ambiguous the accountability, the more visible your leadership opportunity.

1.4.4   Use Language that Reflects Ownership

Words shape perceptions. Leaders who frequently use passive language: *'It happened'*, *'That's not in my scope'*, *'They didn't deliver'* erode trust and initiative. In contrast, leaders who say: *'I take responsibility'*, *'Here's how we'll fix it'*, or *'Let's learn from this'* shift the culture toward empowerment.

A small habit: Audit your language for subtle disowning. Replace it with verbs of agency.

1.4.5   Stay Close to Consequences

Leaders can unconsciously distance themselves from the consequences of their decisions by layering bureaucracy or relying on layers of reports. Ownership requires proximity, not just to data, but to impact. How do decisions affect people? How does a missed deadline ripple into customer dissatisfaction? How does policy affect morale?

A regular practice: Ask direct questions to those affected. Don't manage only from the dashboard, walk the floor.

1.4.6 Take Responsibility Publicly, Share Credit Liberally

One of the most powerful daily behaviours of leaders who manifest ownership is how they respond in success and failure. When failure comes, they don't seek shields; they take the hit. When success arrives, they step back and celebrate others. This reversal builds deep loyalty and trust.

A daily mantra: 'If we fail, it's on me. If we win, it's because of you.'

1.4.7 Make Visible What Others Overlook

Leadership also involves recognising the invisible labour, the subtle signals, and the slow-burning problems others miss. Leaders who truly take ownership learn to see what others often miss, like silent disengagement, team members who feel left out, or hidden ethical concerns.

A conscious act: Pause once a day to ask, '*What am I missing?*' and then go seek it.

1.4.8 Summing Up - Ownership as a Living Practice

Manifesting ownership is not about perfection. It is about posture over position, intent over ego, and consistency over control. In every choice, conversation, and challenge, a leader has the opportunity to ask:

'*What does ownership require of me in this moment?*'

When asked sincerely, and lived consistently, that question becomes a compass for authentic, courageous, and transformational leadership.

1.5 Creating a Culture of Ownership: From Individual Action to Organisational Ethos

While personal ownership is the starting point, sustainable excellence emerges only when ownership becomes systemic. The most resilient and adaptive organisations are not those where ownership is enforced from above, but where it is embraced at every level. In such cultures, people act not out of obligation, but out of identity.

True leadership, then, is not only about manifesting ownership in oneself but about cultivating it in others. It is about moving from individual responsibility to a collective ethos, where ownership is contagious, expected, and celebrated.

1.5.1   From Personal Example to Shared Expectation

Cultures form around what is repeated and what is rewarded. When leaders consistently model ownership in their words, decisions, and behaviours, they create psychological permission for others to do the same.

But modelling alone is not enough. Leaders must also:

Explicitly value ownership in reviews, feedback, and recognition systems.

Challenge disowning language and behaviours wherever they appear.

Provide autonomy - ownership cannot thrive where micromanagement suffocates initiative.

Remove the Fear of Failure

Ownership cannot exist in a culture where mistakes are punished more than they are understood. People do not step up when they fear falling. A culture of ownership is also a culture of safety, where taking initiative, experimenting, and learning from missteps is welcomed.

Leaders must ask:

Are we cultivating courage or compliance?

To grow ownership, failure must be seen not as a defect in character, but as a feature of growth.

1.5.2   Flatten the 'Blame Ladder'

In weak ownership cultures, blame moves upward, responsibility gets deferred downward, and silence fills the middle. In strong cultures, everyone takes initiative, everyone speaks up, and everyone owns outcomes. This happens when hierarchies of fear are replaced by networks of trust.

Encourage upward feedback.

Promote horizontal accountability between peers.

Celebrate 'step-up stories' in real time, not just during annual town halls.

1.5.3   Clarify, But Don't Constrict

Ownership flourishes when roles are clear but flexible. Too much ambiguity creates paralysis. Too much rigidity stifles initiative. Leaders must create a shared understanding of what needs to be done, while allowing flexibility in how it gets done.

A culture of ownership values:

Initiative over instruction

Alignment over compliance

Judgment over procedure

Stories as Cultural Currency

Nothing embeds a culture faster than stories. Stories of someone stepping up when it wasn't their job. Stories of a team turning around a crisis through shared responsibility. Stories of a junior employee who saw a gap, took charge, and made it better.

Leaders should gather, retell, and institutionalise such stories. They are the living proof of what the organisation truly values.

1.5.4 From Individual Ownership to Organisational Identity

When enough people start saying *'I'll take care of it'*, it becomes more than a behaviour; it becomes who we are. And in that transformation lies the power of leadership: to take something internal and personal, and grow it into something collective and enduring.

Creating a culture of ownership is not about creating heroes. It's about making ownership normal; something so woven into the way people think and act, that anything less feels unnatural.

Because in the end, an organisation that waits to be told is always one step behind. But an organisation where everyone acts like an owner is not just prepared for the future; it is already shaping it.

CHAPTER 2

The Ripple Effect of Invisible Decisions

Some of the most impactful leadership decisions are the ones never consciously made. A leader's neglect, hesitation, or failure to engage in a timely manner can set off cascading consequences, much like a stone skipping across water. The danger of these invisible decisions is that they often go unnoticed until they manifest as crises. Leaders must train themselves to identify these decision points before their effects spiral out of control. By cultivating a mindset that accounts for unseen consequences, they move from passive oversight to strategic foresight.

2.1 Leadership isn't Just About the Decisions You Make, But the Ones You Don't Make

2.1.1

Leadership is often glorified as a series of bold decisions: moments of clarity in crisis, daring calls in uncertainty, and courageous stands in adversity. These are the visible hallmarks of leadership that make headlines and echo in boardrooms. But equally powerful, and often more consequential, are the silent moments: the decisions not taken, the issues bypassed, the risks avoided, and the ambiguities left unresolved. These invisible decisions, or non-decisions, don't make the front page, but they write the hidden chapters of an organisation's destiny.

Every leader makes choices, but what truly defines leadership is what one chooses to ignore. The subtle avoidance of a brewing conflict, the convenient delay in resolving a culture issue, the hesitation to address toxic behaviour from a high performer; each of these is a decision cloaked in inaction. And yet, their ripple effects are profound. The vacuum left by indecision becomes fertile ground for ambiguity, erosion of trust, and moral drift.

To not act is to act. To delay a hard call is to decide in favor of the status quo. To avoid confronting an ethical concern is to implicitly endorse it. The illusion that non-action is neutral is among the most dangerous fallacies in leadership. In reality, non-decisions cascade like quiet ripples that often grow into storms; ones the leader may neither have anticipated nor be able to control.

Consider the leader who refuses to intervene in a team's growing dysfunction because addressing it might offend a senior member. Or the executive who chooses not to define a vision, allowing the organisation to drift. These aren't merely passive moments; they're pivotal leadership choices made in silence. The absence of intervention becomes the presence of consent.

This is where ownership becomes inescapable. A leader may not have initiated a crisis, but their failure to act becomes part of the architecture of the problem. Leadership, then, is not merely about taking credit for results or responsibility for visible actions; it's about owning the shadows of one's silence.

The paradox is clear: the more power a leader holds, the more invisible their inaction becomes, and the greater its consequence. The weight of unmade decisions doesn't disappear; it diffuses into culture, corrodes clarity, and compounds complexity. Often, by the time the consequences of a non-decision surface, it's too late to trace them back to their origin.

In truth, the costliest decisions in leadership are rarely the ones boldly taken; they are the ones quietly evaded. And that is why leadership must be practiced not only with strategic foresight but with the moral courage to choose, even when choosing is inconvenient, uncomfortable, or unpopular.

The best leaders do not merely lead by the actions they take, but by the disciplined refusal to let silence become a substitute for decision. They do not see inaction as a safe haven but as a leadership choice that demands the same scrutiny as any other. Because in the end, the legacy of leadership is not just built on what you did; it's also shaped by what you chose not to do, and why.

2.1.2   The Lighthouse That Didn't Turn

Along a rugged coast, there stood an old lighthouse perched high above the crashing waves. For generations, it had guided ships through treacherous waters, its beam slicing through the fog to show the way. It wasn't perfect, but it was dependable. Mariners trusted its rhythm, its reach, and its resolve.

One evening, as a storm was coming in, the lighthouse keeper noticed something strange. The gear that turned the beam was getting stuck. It had slowed, casting light only in one direction. The keeper hesitated. It would take time to fix. He told himself that most ships came from the visible side anyway, and surely the storm wouldn't be too bad. So he let it be, just for the night.

That night, a vessel approached from the blind side. Navigating the darkness, the crew searched for the light that should have been there, but found none. Disoriented, the ship veered off course and ran aground. Lives were lost. Cargo destroyed. The coast, once guided, now bore scars of silence.

The next morning, the lighthouse stood unchanged. No alarms had sounded. No one had seen the decision the keeper didn't make. But the consequences were undeniable.

Leadership is much the same. The light we fail to rotate, thinking it won't matter, or that someone else will notice, can lead others into peril. It is not always the dramatic choices that define us, but the small, silent refusals to act when it counted most.

The cost of inaction is rarely immediate - but always real. The invisible decisions cast the longest shadows.

2.1.3   The Case of Nokia India: The Silence Before the Fall

For years, Nokia was the undisputed leader in India's mobile phone market. By 2007–08, it had achieved a near-monopolistic position, especially in Tier 2 and Tier 3 cities. Its distribution network, brand recall, and durability made it a household name. But what is less discussed is not just the decisions it made, but the ones it didn't.

While the global headquarters in Finland hesitated to embrace the Android operating system, Nokia India remained silent, waiting for clarity rather than challenging headquarters with ground realities. Executives in India could see a rapid shift in consumer expectations. Android phones, especially from Samsung, were penetrating the market with touch-screens, apps, and affordability. Indian customers were evolving, but Nokia India did not escalate, challenge, or adapt in time.

There was a critical non-decision at play: the failure to advocate strongly for change, or to localise product development for an Indian market that was hungry for innovation. As an organisation, they chose not to act fast enough. They didn't pivot. They didn't push back. And they didn't speak up loudly when the writing on the wall was clear.

The silence wasn't about lack of insight; it was about deference, hesitation, and fear of being wrong. And in leadership, especially at the country level, silence in the face of seismic change is a form of abdication.

By the time Nokia attempted to re-enter the market with updated models, it was too late. The Indian consumer had moved on. The ripple effect of invisible decisions, or decisions deferred, was irreversible.

Lesson: Leadership is not only about implementing what's handed down. It's about owning the responsibility to challenge, to escalate, and to act when the moment demands, even if the authority lies elsewhere. Silence is not safety. It is complicity.

2.2   *How Neglect, Deferral, or 'Small Choices' Compound into Larger Consequences*

Responsibility rarely announces itself with fanfare. Often, it begins as a whisper: a nudge to act, to intervene, to decide. Yet when we ignore that whisper, postpone decisions, or dismiss small choices as inconsequential, we set in motion a silent momentum whose true weight is only realised in retrospect. *This is the paradox of compounded neglect:* the choices we believe to be minor are often the ones that shape the major turning points of our lives and organisations.

2.2.1   The Illusion of the Insignificant

We live much of our daily existence in the realm of the 'small', tiny judgments, brief interactions, minor acts of omission. But small does not mean harmless. What appears insignificant today may be the seed of tomorrow's crisis. Neglect is rarely dramatic. It is slow erosion, not a sudden collapse. The machine doesn't break from a single missed maintenance check, but from a dozen skipped ones. Trust doesn't disintegrate overnight, but through a steady drizzle of inattention and postponed accountability.

Every deferred responsibility accumulates unseen interest. When decisions are left unmade, conversations are avoided, and risks are not taken, they do not disappear. Instead, they gather silently in the background until one day they demand to be addressed, often at a greater cost than before.

2.2.2   The Dominoes We Don't Notice

Consider leadership in any domain: family, corporate, or civic. A manager tolerates a slightly toxic behaviour in a high-performing employee, thinking it's not worth addressing yet. A parent repeatedly delays honest conversations with their adolescent child. A policymaker avoids tackling a small irregularity in a system. Each instance is a quiet compromise.

But such tolerance normalises deviance. What starts as an exception becomes the rule. The invisible choices ripple outwards. They influence culture. They shape precedents. They create blind spots. When responsibility is not taken early, the burden does not disappear. It quietly falls on those who come after, whether they are team members, citizens, or future generations.

2.2.3   Deferred Ownership Is Not Abdicated Ownership

Here lies the heart of the paradox: in deferring ownership, we do not escape it; we merely shift its timing and its terms. The price must still be paid, only now with added compound consequences. In avoiding the small discomfort of the present, we invite larger pain in the future. And by the time it arrives, the cost is rarely borne by the deferrer alone; it spills over to others, often unfairly.

Leadership, then, is not just about the bold moves or grand strategies. It is also about the quiet discipline of showing up, about taking responsibility for the small, the ordinary, and the things that seem unimportant. It is about resisting the temptation to say, *'It can wait'*, when your conscience says, *'Act now.'*

2.2.4   The Silent Shapers of Destiny

Histories, personal and collective, are not only shaped by what was done but equally by what was not. Wars have erupted not only due to aggression but also due to prolonged inaction. Relationships fracture not only from betrayal but from chronic neglect. Organisations fail not only from bad strategy but from deferred decisions and unacknowledged truths.

Thus, we must begin to see our small choices as sacred, not because each is grand in itself, but because their cumulative effect is monumental. The question isn't whether our choices have consequences, but whether we are conscious of the chain they begin to form.

In the paradox of inescapable ownership, even our silence speaks. Even our pause moves the needle. And often, the most lasting legacy of our leadership lies not in the visible decisions we made, but in the invisible ones we avoided.

2.2.5   Examples

Example 1: The Bhopal Gas Tragedy – A Case of Compounded Neglect

One of the most devastating industrial disasters in history, the Bhopal Gas Tragedy of 1984, stands as a stark reminder of how neglect, deferral, and 'small' choices can accumulate into irreversible catastrophe. At its core, the tragedy was not caused by a single, dramatic failure but by a series of ignored warnings, deferred maintenance, underestimation of risk, and lack of proactive ownership across multiple levels of responsibility.

The Union Carbide plant in Bhopal was already known for its declining safety standards. Key safety systems - such as the refrigeration unit meant to keep the lethal methyl isocyanate (MIC) cool, the gas scrubber to neutralise leaks, and the flare tower to burn escaping gas - had either been shut down, poorly maintained, or were inoperable at the time of the disaster. Each of these was a seemingly cost-saving, operationally expedient choice made over time. No one decision caused the disaster; rather, the compounding of small oversights did.

Even more troubling was the absence of a culture of ownership. Employees had raised safety concerns, but management deferred decisive action. Government oversight bodies had limited enforcement, and even local authorities lacked complete awareness of the plant's dangers. Responsibility was scattered just enough for each actor to claim plausible deniability, but not enough for anyone to take decisive action. The result was devastating. More than 15,000 lives were lost by conservative estimates, hundreds of thousands were injured, and an ecological and legal tragedy still hangs heavy on India's conscience.

This tragedy is not merely a historical footnote. It is a profound illustration of what happens when small decisions are seen in isolation and responsibility is deferred in the hope that someone else will eventually step in. In reality, no one ever does. Ownership, when inescapable, returns with compounded consequences.

The Bhopal case teaches us that leadership is not simply about responding to crisis but about recognising its early shadows. It is about understanding that neglect, especially of 'minor' issues, has a trajectory. And that trajectory is rarely benign.

Example 2: The Snowball Effect: The Rise and Fall of Kingfisher Airlines

The story of Kingfisher Airlines is often narrated as a tale of flamboyance and ambition gone awry. But beneath the surface, it is a case study in how a series of seemingly small decisions - ignored warnings, unchecked indulgences, and delayed corrections - cascaded into one of the most prominent corporate failures in modern India.

When Kingfisher Airlines launched in 2005, it entered the aviation market with glamour, luxury, and high expectations. But beneath the premium branding lay a business model fraught with vulnerabilities from the very beginning:

a. Aggressive expansion without consolidation of routes was justified in the name of market dominance.

b. Merging with the loss-making Air Deccan, aimed at fast-tracking international operations, was a strategic gamble taken without adequate risk assessment.

c. Excessive investment in luxury and customer experience-while appreciated-was unsustainable for the cost-sensitive Indian market.

d. Mounting debt, initially seen as manageable, was rolled over repeatedly instead of being rationalised.

Each of these decisions, in isolation, seemed defensible - bold, even. But their cumulative impact formed a snowball that began to roll downhill, silently picking up mass and speed. What was missing was not intelligence, but restraint; not ambition, but accountability.

As losses mounted and operational missteps accumulated, the company entered a cycle of financial strain, employee unrest, creditor pressure, and eventually regulatory crackdown. Kingfisher's flying license was suspended in 2012. Salaries went unpaid. Debts to banks, over ₹9,000 crore, were left unpaid. And the collapse rippled beyond one company; it shook the trust in private airline governance and raised questions about the robustness of India's banking due diligence mechanisms.

The Snowball Effect here was not triggered by a single catastrophic event. It was the result of multiple overlooked decisions, deferred reality checks, and delayed responsibility. By the time accountability was enforced, it was too late for recovery and too costly for the ecosystem that had enabled the slide.

This example drives home a brutal truth: leadership that indulges in continual postponement of hard decisions eventually becomes incapable of reversing its own momentum. The snowball doesn't stop because the slope was gentle. It stops only when it crashes.

2.2.6   The Unseen Gravity of Our Smallest Steps

In life and leadership alike, it is rarely the grand decisions that derail us; it is the subtle ones we overlook. A delay here, a compromise there, a silence chosen over truth; they gather mass like a snowball on a quiet slope. By the time the descent becomes visible, momentum has already turned irreversible.

The paradox lies in this: the smallest choices are the easiest to make, and the easiest to dismiss. But they are not weightless. They are the moral molecules of our character, the ethical architecture of our institutions. What we defer today does not disappear, it simply waits, quietly gathering consequence.

Just as a river shapes a canyon not through a single flood but by persistent flow, so too do our lives and legacies take shape: not through one defining moment, but through a thousand invisible ones.

True ownership begins not with dramatic declarations but with an intimate awareness of how every act, especially the inconspicuous, has direction and destiny.

2.3   *Framework for Recognising and Responding to Invisible Decisions Before They Become Crisis*

In leadership, the most dangerous decisions are often the ones never consciously made. They manifest not in loud declarations, but in silent defaults - unspoken compromises, habitual postponements, and systemic blind spots. These invisible decisions may seem benign, but they quietly shape culture, erode standards, and compound neglect until crisis becomes inevitable.

This framework helps leaders surface and respond to these subtle signals before they solidify into irreversible patterns. It combines intuitive insight with practical tools for diagnosis and action.

Frame 1. The 'Low Friction, High Frequency' Filter: Micro-Compromises with Macro Impact

What choices feel too small to challenge, yet happen too often to ignore?

Seemingly minor acts - approving without reading, deferring difficult conversations, tolerating subpar performance - often go unchallenged because they require little effort or conflict. But when these low-friction choices repeat, they compound into cultural drift and unspoken norms of mediocrity.

Red Flags

- Repeated acceptance of subpar work
- 'Low priority' tags that keep resurfacing
- Feedback that is softened or withheld

Frame 2. The 'Patterns of Postponement': Delay as a Form of Neglect

Are we normalising delay under the guise of prioritisation?

When decisions are perpetually deferred, and issues are parked for 'future resolution' that never comes, a culture of avoidance forms. This is not mere delay; it's passive resistance to ownership and an unconscious belief that time will solve what accountability won't.

Red Flags

- Unfinished action points that persist across meetings
- Chronic rescheduling of critical decisions
- Meetings that conclude with *'let's revisit this'* without follow-through

Frame 3. The 'Nobody Owns This' Zone: The Grey Areas of Accountability

Which tasks fall between roles, remaining unresolved?

Invisible decisions often fester in spaces where responsibility is ambiguous. Without clear ownership, even critical issues are allowed to drift. Over time, these grey zones create bottlenecks and blame cycles that infect performance and morale.

Red Flags

- Chronic delays or reassignments
- Blame without resolution
- Work-streams with unclear or rotating ownership

Frame 4. The 'Silent Shrug' Signal: Mistaking Silence for Alignment

Where is disengagement masquerading as consensus?

When people stop questioning, especially those who used to, it's rarely a sign of agreement. More often, it reflects disillusionment or fear, an internal decision to withdraw rather than speak. Silence becomes complicity in decline.

Red Flags

- Absence of dissent in high-stakes meetings
- Passive acceptance of flawed plans
- Corridor conversations replacing open forums

Frame 5. The 'Tolerance for Mediocrity' Trap: When Standards Become Negotiable

Are we excusing underperformance to avoid discomfort?

Each time mediocrity is tolerated, a silent policy is enacted: one that says excellence is optional. What begins as small allowances quickly hardens into cultural norms where shortcuts thrive and improvement stalls.

Red Flags

- Errors dismissed with 'it's okay'
- Rewarding speed over quality
- Low-performing team members not held accountable

Frame 6. The 'Short-Term Relief, Long-Term Cost' Trade-off

What decisions bring comfort today but build debt tomorrow?

Rushed fixes and hasty approvals may offer temporary relief, but they accrue technical, financial, and moral debt. Over time, these decisions manifest as chronic firefighting, exhausted teams, and missed strategic goals.

Red Flags

- Crisis-driven culture
- Leaders constantly in reactive mode
- Little time for reflection, prevention, or innovation

Frame 7. The 'Historical Inertia' Check: Legacy Practices That Outlive Their Use

Are we doing this because it's right, or just because it's familiar?

Practices passed down unquestioned can become invisible decisions made by default. When teams fail to reassess habits, they become captives of outdated playbooks.

Red Flags

- Repetitive routines with unclear value
- Phrases like 'this is how we've always done it'
- Resistance to experimentation or change

Frame 8. The 'Discomfort You Can't Quite Name': Intuition as a Leadership Sensor

What's your gut telling you beyond the data?

Intuitive discomfort often precedes measurable dysfunction. A shift in tone, body language, or team energy can be the first sign that something vital is off. Conscious leaders don't dismiss these cues; they investigate them.

Red Flags

- Persistent unease without obvious cause
- Emotional fatigue or team cynicism
- A growing sense of disconnection from purpose or people

The Invisible Decisions → Crisis Loop

Unattended invisible decisions → Cultural Drift → Compounding Neglect → Sudden Crisis

How to Use This Framework

Diagnose: Regularly review decisions, habits, and conversations through these lenses.

Discuss: Create safe spaces for teams to voice early concerns and reflect on 'invisible' choices.

Decide: Take conscious corrective action, early, openly, and consistently.

<u>Final Reflection</u>

The difference between breakdown and breakthrough often lies in our ability to notice what others overlook. Leadership is not only about solving the visible, but sensing the invisible. This framework is not just a tool; it's a mindset.

'Conscious leadership isn't about reacting to crisis. It's about reading the whispers before they become screams.'

2.4   *Cultivating Conscious Accountability in the Invisible Moments*

Responsibility, when visible, is easy to claim. Taking credit for success, showing up in a crisis, or making bold statements from the frontlines; these are moments when ownership is expected, even celebrated.

True leadership is built in the quiet moments, in those seemingly small instances when there is no spotlight, no applause, and no one is watching.

This is where conscious accountability begins.

2.4.1   Micro-Decisions as Moral Anchors

Every day is filled with hundreds of small choices. *Do you respond to that email now or later? Do you acknowledge a mistake or brush it aside? Do you check a fact or assume it's accurate?* These are not trivial acts; they are compounding signals of who we are becoming.

Leaders who excel in the invisible moments recognise that every micro-decision is a moral anchor. It either reinforces integrity or dilutes it.

Over time, this accumulation shapes culture more than any mission statement ever could.

John C. Maxwell: 'Small disciplines repeated with consistency every day lead to great achievements gained slowly over time.'

2.4.2 The Practice of Presence

Neglect doesn't always come from intent. Often, it is a by-product of distraction. In a world of endless noise, leaders must cultivate the rare ability to be fully present. To listen with attention. To notice what is unsaid. To pause before reacting.

Presence is not passive; it's a discipline. It allows a leader to detect the shift in a teammate's tone, the hesitation in a decision, the recurring friction in a system. And it is in these subtle shifts that course corrections begin.

Presence turns the invisible into the visible.

2.4.3 Creating a Culture of Invitation, Not Imposition

True accountability cannot be enforced; it must be invited. Cultures where people willingly take ownership are built not through pressure, but through trust and modelling.

This means:

Leaders who admit their own mistakes publicly.

Teams where questions are rewarded, not punished.

Systems where feedback flows upward, not just downward.

When individuals feel psychologically safe, they take responsibility not only for what they are told to do, but for what needs to be done.

2.4.4   The Discipline of Daily Debrief

One powerful tool for nurturing invisible accountability is the practice of daily self-reflection. A simple end-of-day question: *'Where did I show up today, and where did I turn away?'* can be transformative.

It doesn't require public confession. Just honest attention. The aim is not perfection, but pattern recognition. Over time, these micro-adjustments become part of the leader's inner compass.

What is inspected privately is corrected permanently.

2.4.5   Transcending Transactional Thinking

At its root, accountability thrives when we move beyond transactional thinking: *'What am I required to do?'* to transformational thinking: *'What am I capable of contributing?'*

This shift reframes invisible moments not as obligations, but as opportunities. To elevate a conversation. To prevent harm. To speak for someone unheard. To resolve a tension no one has yet named.

Such acts rarely make headlines. But they make cultures. They are the invisible hands that shape visible outcomes.

2.4.6   Leadership That Begins Before It Is Needed

To be truly accountable is to take ownership not because the world demands it, but because one's conscience does. It is to lead before the spotlight, before the crisis, before the applause.

Invisible leadership is the ultimate paradox: what no one sees, everyone feels.

2.5   *The Tipping Point of Unclaimed Responsibility*

Responsibility that is delayed doesn't disappear. It migrates.

When the individual neglects, the team absorbs. When the team avoids, the system absorbs. When the system denies, reality intervenes. And reality is the most unforgiving auditor; its books always balance, often through collapse.

This is the quiet yet inevitable turning point of unclaimed responsibility. It is the moment when what was once manageable spreads beyond control, when the unseen weight of avoidance becomes too obvious to ignore.

2.5.1   The System Doesn't Break - It Reveals

Most crises in organisations, institutions, and even societies do not erupt suddenly. They reveal themselves after long incubation periods. What appears to be a breakdown is often a delayed revelation of what was already broken but unaddressed.

A collapsed bridge often tells a story of ignored maintenance logs.

A failing company often carries years of unheeded audits or muffled employee feedback.

A national scandal is usually preceded by whispers, whistleblowers, and willful blindness.

Before every implosion, there is a moment when someone saw the crack, and walked away.

This is not fate. This is design, accidental, yes, but engineered nonetheless through cumulative neglect and convenient silence.

2.5.2   The Boiling Point Is a Process, Not a Moment

Much like water doesn't boil the moment heat is applied, systems do not fail in the moment of collapse. They inch toward it. Slowly. Predictably. Sometimes even visibly, but only to those willing to look.

The tipping point is not when the consequences arrive. It is when they become uncontainable, when there are no buffers left to absorb the cost.

Consider:

The growing fatigue of a stretched team that finally results in mass attrition.

The snowballing of a product flaw that erupts into reputational damage.

The cumulative emotional suppression in a relationship that bursts into irreversible silence.

All of these are not sudden failures; they are slow-motion accountability gaps finally reaching terminal velocity.

2.5.3   The Leader's Burden and Blessing

The true weight of leadership lies not in carrying outcomes, but in sensing and owning the drift before it becomes a downfall. Leaders who understand this paradox cultivate a long-view awareness, an ability to sense not just the pulse of the present, but the trajectory of what's being ignored.

They ask:

What truth are we avoiding because it is uncomfortable?

Whose silence is a signal?

Which unresolved issue, if left unattended, could become irreversible?

They do not wait for accountability to be assigned. They assume it. Because unclaimed responsibility is not just a lapse; it's a liability in waiting.

2.5.4   The Unseen Tipping Becomes the Visible Toppling

The ultimate tragedy is not that systems collapse; it is that their collapse was often preventable.

Responsibility, when avoided long enough, finds its way back through consequence. The cost of unclaimed responsibility is never borne by the one who denied it alone; it ripples, it expands, and eventually, it engulfs.

The tipping point is not a failure of intelligence. It is a failure of ownership.

2.6   *Summary: The Ripple Becomes the Wave*

In this chapter, we explored how leadership is not only tested in visible crises, but more crucially shaped in the quiet spaces of everyday decisions, the invisible moments where accountability can either be owned or outsourced.

We saw how neglect, deferral, and 'small choices' often compound into large consequences, creating ripples that eventually become tidal waves. Through the lens of the Snowball Effect, we examined how cultures and systems inherit the weight of unattended decisions.

We then turned our focus inward, on recognising early warning signals, the quiet normalisation of delay, the slow death of dissent, and the discomfort we often ignore. These subtle patterns are not noise; they are signs. And leaders who learn to read them can course-correct before consequences harden into collapse.

Finally, we arrived at the Tipping Point of Unclaimed Responsibility, the moment when the accumulation of avoidance becomes too heavy to contain, when systems break not from sudden pressure, but from prolonged silence.

At its heart, this chapter calls us to a deeper awareness:

What we ignore privately returns publicly. What we defer internally manifests externally. And what we fail to own in time, will eventually own us.

True leadership, then, begins not with action, but with attention to the invisible choices that write the visible story of consequence.

CHAPTER 3

When Taking Responsibility is a Strategic Mistake

Accountability is a cornerstone of great leadership, but taking too much responsibility can weaken an organisation. When leaders assume sole ownership over every outcome, they inadvertently promote dependency, discourage initiative, and create bottlenecks. A more effective approach is to strike a balance, knowing when to step forward and when to empower others. True leadership lies not in carrying every burden but in distributing responsibility wisely. This ensures resilience, promotes autonomy, and ultimately strengthens the collective ability to solve problems.

3.1 Are There Times When Saying 'The Buck Stops with Me' Can Harm an Organisation?

The phrase 'the buck stops with me' is often celebrated as the ultimate mark of responsible leadership. It exudes strength, integrity, and a sense of moral clarity. Leaders who embrace this mindset position themselves as shields, absorbing blame, criticism, and accountability so their teams can move forward unencumbered. However, like many virtues taken to extremes or misapplied in the wrong context, even this noble sentiment can become counterproductive.

There are times when an overemphasis on personal ownership, particularly in hierarchical or complex systems, can stifle initiative, obscure systemic flaws, and paradoxically harm the very culture of responsibility it aims to promote.

3.1.1 The Problem of Overcentralisation

When a leader repeatedly declares that all responsibility stops with them, it can inadvertently centralise not just blame, but decision-making and initiative. Subordinates may grow passive, waiting for the leader to take charge or solve issues, leading to a dangerous culture of dependency. In this environment, individuals are less likely to speak up, challenge the status quo, or take proactive steps, because the unspoken understanding is that the final word (and therefore the risk) lies with someone else.

Over time, this stifles the development of leadership at all levels. Talented individuals may feel disempowered, creativity may decline, and the organisation becomes more brittle, relying on a single person to bear the weight of collective judgment and decision-making.

3.1.2 Masking Systemic Failures

Saying 'the buck stops with me' can also become a strategic mistake when it shields the organisation from acknowledging deeper, structural flaws. If a major failure is chalked up solely to a leader's misjudgment, it may allow systemic inefficiencies, misaligned incentives, or toxic team dynamics to go unexamined. The issue is framed as a failure of personal judgment rather than a failure of design.

In such cases, the leader's noble gesture of assuming blame diverts attention from learning opportunities. The system does not improve; it merely resets with a new figure at the helm. True responsibility must sometimes be distributed, not diluted, across the organisation to ensure sustainable growth and genuine learning.

3.1.3 Encouraging Hero Syndrome

Some leaders wear the mantra of ultimate responsibility as a badge of honour, but underneath, it may mask a subtle form of ego. The desire to be seen as the one who takes the fall, who always steps in, can become performative. It feeds the 'hero syndrome', the belief that the leader must rescue the organisation from every crisis, thus denying the team the chance to grow through adversity.

While admirable in crisis moments, this approach can be corrosive in the long term. Organisations become over-reliant on heroic interventions rather than building systems, processes, and cultures that can prevent crises in the first place.

3.1.4   A Case for Shared Ownership

Strategic leadership is not about absorbing all blame; it is about architecting a system of distributed accountability. In high-performing teams, ownership is not something one person hoards. It is something that circulates. Each team member understands their sphere of influence, their domain of control, and the shared values that guide decision-making.

In such environments, leaders don't just say *'the buck stops with me.'* They say, *'Let's examine where the buck truly belongs'*: not to deflect blame, but to allocate responsibility intelligently. Ownership becomes a tool for organisational learning, not just personal valour.

3.1.5   Responsibility as a Lever, Not a Shield

There is a profound difference between using responsibility as a shield and wielding it as a lever. A leader who habitually says 'the buck stops with me' might earn respect in the short term, but in the long term, may hinder the development of a resilient, adaptive organisation. True leadership lies in knowing when to take the fall, and when to step aside and allow others to rise by owning their part of the journey.

The paradox is clear: absolute responsibility can sometimes be a dereliction of duty if it silences learning, discourages initiative, or masks collective shortcomings. Responsibility must not always stop at one person; it must ripple through the system.

3.1.6   Examples

Example 1: The Fall of Nokia – When Responsibility Was Over-Centralised

In the early 2000s, Nokia was the undisputed leader in the mobile phone industry. Its dominance seemed unshakable; until it wasn't. By the end of the decade, Nokia had lost significant market share to Apple and Android-powered smartphones. Much has been written about the technical, strategic, and marketing missteps that led to Nokia's decline. But one of the less visible causes was the failure of distributed responsibility within the company's leadership structure.

Nokia's then-CEO, Olli-Pekka Kallasvuo, was known for taking personal responsibility for the company's direction. He emphasised top-down control and often made key strategic decisions in a tight circle of executives. While this style may have worked during Nokia's heyday, it became a critical weakness when the market shifted rapidly.

Middle management, though aware of growing internal dysfunction, especially the lack of agility and the slow response to software trends, was often reluctant to raise red flags. A culture of fear had taken root. The 'buck' effectively stopped at the top, but not in an empowering way; it stopped progress from bubbling up.

After Nokia's smartphone operating system strategy faltered, many of the CEO's decisions were criticised. Kallasvuo took personal responsibility for the company's struggles, but by then, the damage was systemic. Talented engineers and product managers had long felt their voices didn't matter. Responsibility hadn't been shared; it had been siloed.

When Stephen Elop took over as CEO in 2010, his infamous 'Burning Platform' memo acknowledged not only the failures but also the urgent need for cultural transformation. But it was too late. Nokia's inability to distribute ownership, encourage dissenting views, and allow bottom-up innovation had cost it the market leadership.

This episode illustrates the paradox vividly: when responsibility is over-centralised in the name of leadership, it can cause an organisation to lose its adaptive capacity. The heroic acceptance of blame may look noble, but in reality, it often hides deeper cultural fractures.

Example 2: Jet Airways – When Singular Leadership Became a Strategic Liability

Jet Airways was once India's premier private airline, admired for its service quality, operational reach, and loyal customer base. However, its dramatic downfall in 2019 offers a compelling case of how over-personalised leadership and a concentration of control can turn the noble idea of 'the buck stops with me' into an organisational blindfold.

Naresh Goyal, the founder and long-time Chairman of Jet Airways, was known for his hands-on management style. While this approach helped the airline take off in the 1990s and early 2000s, it later became a constraint. Key decisions, from fleet expansion and route selection to financial structuring, remained tightly held within the top leadership circle, often without robust institutional checks or shared strategic ownership across departments.

When the airline began facing mounting financial stress due to rising fuel costs, intense competition, and flawed pricing strategies, Goyal continued to project confidence and absorbed public responsibility. He appeared to hold ultimate control, but beneath the surface, dissenting voices were either muted or ignored. Professional managers often found themselves overruled, and many capable leaders left the company, sensing a lack of space for independent thinking.

Even when lenders and investors suggested changes in governance structures and operational transparency, Goyal reportedly resisted relinquishing control. By the time he stepped down in 2019, it was too late. Jet Airways had grounded operations, thousands of employees were left without jobs, and creditors scrambled to recover their dues.

The tragedy was not only in financial losses; it was in the stifling of a potentially resilient organisation under the weight of one man's refusal to decentralise responsibility. Goyal repeatedly shouldered the burden, but that ownership, instead of being strategic, became emotional and possessive.

The lesson? Leadership that clings to 'the buck stops with me' without empowering others becomes a bottleneck in disguise. Responsibility, to be effective, must travel-through minds, teams, and systems. Otherwise, it risks becoming the last word, when what's really needed is a shared conversation.

3.1.7   Reflection: Responsibility That Doesn't Travel, Fails to Transform

The instinct to say 'the buck stops with me' often comes from a place of integrity. It signals that the leader is willing to stand in the storm. But storms are not weathered by posture; they are weathered by preparation, participation, and the collective strength of the ship and crew.

In both global and Indian contexts, from Nokia to Jet Airways, we see that over-centralising responsibility in one person, no matter how committed or capable, eventually isolates the leader and weakens the organisation. It breeds a culture of learned helplessness, where people hesitate to take initiative because they're not sure if it's their place to do so.

The true danger lies in the illusion that ownership equals control. But in today's volatile, complex world, strategic ownership is not about control; it's about orchestration. Leaders must know when to absorb pressure and when to deflect it back into the system as constructive accountability.

3.1.8 Principle for Leaders

Don't just stop the buck, circulate it.

Create mechanisms of shared ownership where responsibility becomes everyone's language, not just the leader's legacy.

Distribute decision-making authority, build feedback loops, empower voices across levels, and encourage critical thinking. Own the design of the system more than its day-to-day outcomes. That's where real transformation begins.

In the paradox of inescapable ownership, the wisest leader is not the one who clutches responsibility, but the one who ensures it flows with clarity, courage, and continuity.

3.2 *How Over-Responsibility Can Create Dependency, Stifle Initiative, and Weaken Teams*

Let us dive deeper into the topic we just discussed. *There exists a curious paradox in leadership:* one where the noble intent to take ownership becomes the very force that inhibits growth, weakens teams, and nurtures dependency. While responsible leadership is foundational to organisational success, over-responsibility, when one assumes excessive control or accountability for outcomes, can lead to unintended strategic consequences. Like a parent who never lets their child fall or fail, such leadership can produce teams that are technically functional but psychologically dependent.

3.2.1 The Dependency Trap: When Others Stop Thinking

At first glance, a leader who consistently steps in to solve problems may appear highly competent, even heroic. But this brand of over-responsibility conditions team members to look upward for answers instead of inward. It breeds learned helplessness. The more the leader intervenes, the less incentive there is for others to take initiative, make decisions, or learn from experience.

This creates a top-heavy structure where all roads lead to one person. Bottlenecks emerge. People stop preparing because they assume someone else will step in. In such environments, accountability gets outsourced, not owned. Over time, teams start waiting for direction, for correction, for rescue. This is not empowerment. It is quiet erosion masked as control.

3.2.2 Initiative is Suffocated in the Shade of Over-Ownership

Innovation, problem-solving, and leadership at all levels are only possible when individuals feel both empowered and expected to take charge. But when a leader hovers too close, acting as the perpetual answer-giver and solution-provider, initiative dies a silent death. Talented individuals begin to self-censor. They calculate that the effort of trying (and potentially failing) is less rewarding than deferring to the over-responsible leader.

Over time, such environments discourage experimentation and risk-taking. The result? Teams that appear disciplined but are internally rigid, unable to pivot or respond without approval. The organisation becomes compliant, not creative; precise, but not proactive.

3.2.3 The Hidden Cost: A Weak and Unsustainable Team

In ecosystems where the leader carries the lion's share of responsibility, the team's capacity stagnates. The development of future leaders is delayed, if not entirely derailed. Trust deteriorates, not because people dislike the leader, but because they don't trust themselves anymore.

What starts as a strength becomes a liability. A team that lacks distributed ownership cannot scale. It collapses when the over-responsible leader burns out, leaves, or can no longer play the rescuer.

Even worse, such teams often develop resentment. What begins as gratitude toward the leader's involvement transforms into irritation at being micromanaged. Over-responsibility gradually cultivates under-performance. And in the long run, it hollows out the team's will, pride, and sense of purpose.

3.2.4 The Strategic Insight: Share Ownership, Build Strength

Paradoxically, the strongest leaders are not those who hold the most responsibility, but those who intentionally distribute it. They resist the urge to do everything themselves, even when it is easier or faster. They ask questions instead of giving answers. They step back so others can step up.

Great teams are not created by heroic effort but by the courage to let others own the outcome. Leadership, at its best, is not about proving one's indispensability; it is about making oneself less essential over time.

3.2.5 Case Study: The Over-Responsibility of the Founder – Cafe Coffee Day

Cafe Coffee Day (CCD), once India's most recognisable homegrown coffee chain, rose to prominence under the dynamic leadership of its founder, V.G. Siddhartha. He was a visionary entrepreneur who built a sprawling empire from scratch. But over the years, his deep personal involvement in every critical decision, ranging from financial structuring to expansion strategy, created a system that revolved almost entirely around him.

Despite having built a capable organisation, Siddhartha remained the singular pillar on which everything rested. Key decisions were centralised. The culture, though vibrant, lacked robust decentralisation. Senior management deferred to him, even on operational matters. His personal guarantees were tied to business loans, and financial risk management stayed closely held.

This intense ownership, while admirable in intent, bred dependency within the organisation and among lenders. It stifled the emergence of alternative leadership voices. When financial pressures mounted, owing to liquidity issues, growing debt, and aggressive expansion, the lack of distributed responsibility and internal resilience became evident.

In 2019, his tragic demise shocked the business world. But even more revealing was how vulnerable the organisation was in his absence. The company struggled to navigate forward, not merely because of external challenges, but because internal initiative had been stifled by long-standing over-responsibility at the top.

The CCD episode serves as a painful lesson in the cost of over-centralised ownership. It underscores how excessive responsibility, even when carried with noble intention, can create fragile systems. A founder who does not deliberately build successors or delegate decision-making creates an unsustainable legacy.

3.2.6 Mahabharat: Yudhishthir's Over-Responsibility in the Game of Dice

Yudhishthir, the eldest of the Pandavs, is often admired for his steadfast commitment to dharm and personal responsibility. But even virtues, when stretched beyond balance, become blind spots. His fateful decision to participate in the Dyut Sabha, the game of dice, illustrates a moment where over-responsibility clouded judgement and enabled catastrophic consequences.

Bound by his sense of royal duty and adherence to the Kshatriya code, Yudhishthir felt compelled to accept the invitation to the gambling hall. But once inside, he took it upon himself to keep honouring the rules of the game, wagering one asset after another, even his kingdom, his brothers, himself, and eventually Draupadi.

He assumed full responsibility for upholding the perceived dharm of a guest and a king, but in doing so, he completely overrode his responsibility to his family, his people, and his own judgment. Not once did he stop the game or consult his brothers. No one else stepped in. His sense of individual duty consumed collective wisdom. The silence of the elders in the hall, including Bhishm and Dron, further reflected how over-responsibility by one can lead to under-responsibility by all.

The aftermath was exile, humiliation, and war, a price the entire kingdom had to pay. Yudhishthir's noble virtue became a tragic flaw when he took too much on himself and failed to share ownership or call upon the collective conscience.

This episode is a reminder: *when a leader assumes sole responsibility, they inadvertently disempower others. A shared crisis demands shared courage, not solitary sacrifice.*

3.3 *Leadership Model that Distinguishes When to Own It and When to Distribute Ownership Wisely*

True leadership is not about carrying the world on one's shoulders; it is about knowing when to lift, when to let others lift, and when to simply watch without interference. The challenge is not in owning or delegating, but in knowing when and how to do either.

Over-responsibility is the silent killer of initiative. Under-responsibility is the seedbed of chaos. The paradox lies in navigating the narrow bridge between the two without slipping into either extreme. For this, leaders need a model, not of control, but of discernment. Below is a framework called the Ownership Discernment Matrix, which helps leaders calibrate their actions based on contextual clarity, team maturity, and strategic intent.

3.3.1   The Ownership Discernment Matrix

This model rests on two primary axes:

- Criticality of the Outcome (Low to High)
- Capability of the Team (Low to High)

The combination of these creates four quadrants:

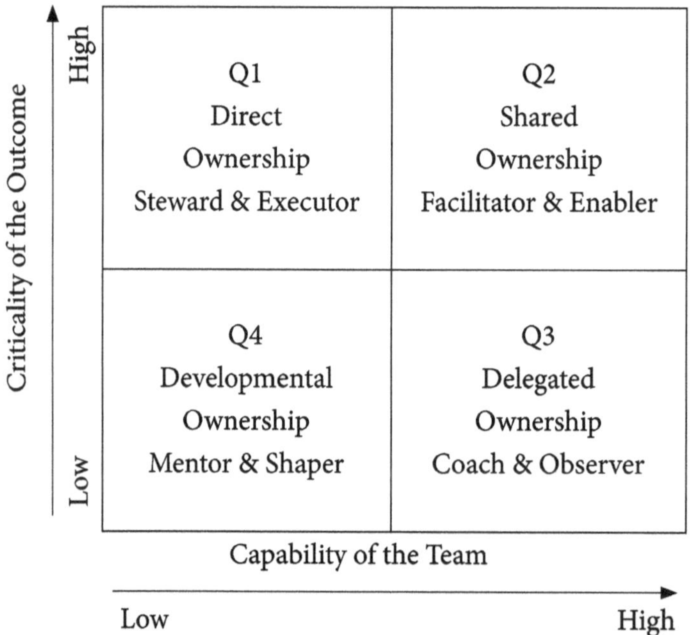

Ownership Discernment Matrix

Quadrant 1. High Outcome Criticality & Low Team Capability → Direct Ownership

Role of the Leader: Steward & Executor

In moments of crisis, high stakes, or when the team is still unseasoned, the leader must own the outcome visibly and fully. This is not micromanagement but strategic stewardship. The leader leads from the front, makes key decisions, and acts as the final firewall. Ownership here is non-negotiable, not for glory, but for the survival or success of the whole.

Example: A ship's captain navigating through a storm does not delegate decision-making.

Quadrant 2. High Outcome Criticality & High Team Capability → Shared Ownership

Role of the Leader: Facilitator & Enabler

When the stakes are high but the team is competent, shared ownership becomes not just possible but powerful. The leader creates clarity of purpose, aligns roles, and monitors progress, but doesn't hover. Responsibility is distributed intelligently, allowing individuals to step up while the leader retains oversight.

This is the ideal state of mature teams: high trust, high stakes, and high performance.

Example: A battle-ready navy team executing a mission where each officer leads a segment with full trust.

Quadrant 3. Low Outcome Criticality & High Team Capability → Delegated Ownership

Role of the Leader: Coach & Observer

Here, the leader has the opportunity to cultivate leadership within the team. Mistakes, if any, are learning moments rather than fatal errors.

By stepping back, the leader sends a signal: *'I trust you'*. This nurtures innovation, autonomy, and accountability.

Example: Letting a junior officer lead a simulation exercise to develop command skills.

Quadrant 4. Low Outcome Criticality & Low Team Capability → Developmental Ownership

Role of the Leader: Mentor & Shaper

Even if outcomes are not mission-critical, the moment is ripe for learning. The leader takes a coaching role, guiding rather than dictating, offering feedback rather than control. This quadrant is ideal for building confidence and capability in young or inexperienced team members.

Example: Assigning a new recruit to manage logistics for a minor port visit, with check-ins and mentorship.

Principles Behind the Matrix

The discernment model is not about convenience; it's about strategic alignment of leadership behaviour with team readiness and task importance. It rests on three essential principles:

Clarity of Intent – Why you choose to own or delegate must serve the larger mission, not your ego or fear.

Continuum of Trust – Distributing ownership is directly proportional to the trust you place in people's growth.

Outcome vs. Ownership Balance – The goal is never to avoid accountability but to amplify outcomes through collective responsibility.

3.3.2   The Invisible Art: Knowing When to Shift

Ownership is not static. A leader must continually reassess the quadrant a situation falls in. A high-criticality task may become low over time. A low-capability team may grow competent. The mastery lies in making the shift fluidly, knowing when to own it, and when to gift ownership to others as an act of empowerment.

In other words, wise leadership is not about always carrying the torch, but knowing when to pass it, how to pass it, and whom to pass it to, without ever letting the flame die.

3.3.3 Case Studies

<u>Case Study 1: Satya Nadella's Leadership Shift at Microsoft</u>

Context

When Satya Nadella became CEO of Microsoft in 2014, the tech giant was losing its edge. Innovation had stagnated, internal silos crippled collaboration, and the once-dominant company had fallen behind in mobile and cloud computing. The situation was high in outcome criticality, but the leadership team was burdened with outdated mindsets and low collective agility - a classic Quadrant 1: Direct Ownership scenario.

Phase 1: Direct Ownership – Leading the Cultural Reset

Satya took direct ownership of Microsoft's cultural transformation. He did not delegate the task of redefining the company's purpose; he authored it. His now-famous rallying cry, 'Hit Refresh', became both metaphor and method. He pushed for a growth mindset across the company, emphasising empathy, learning, and openness.

He made bold decisions, restructuring product lines, redefining success metrics, and initiating a performance review overhaul that rewarded collaboration instead of internal competition.

Leadership Role: Steward & Executor

Nadella owned the reset because only a visible and committed top leader could shift deeply ingrained behaviours. At this point, the team lacked alignment and capability to drive such change independently.

Phase 2: Shared Ownership – Cloud Strategy Execution

Once the new culture took root, Nadella pivoted to shared ownership in rolling out Microsoft's Azure cloud platform. His trust in leaders like Scott Guthrie (Cloud & AI Group) was evident. Guthrie and his team were empowered to make critical architectural and business decisions while Nadella ensured strategic alignment with long-term vision.

Azure's success came not from Nadella's micromanagement but from empowering strong teams to act decisively, while he maintained a birds-eye view.

Leadership Role: Facilitator & Enabler

The outcome was still critical, but the team was now capable. Nadella shifted from being the sole architect to a co-creator.

Phase 3: Delegated Ownership – Developer Ecosystem and LinkedIn Integration

With the company now stabilised and strategic clarity restored, Nadella began delegating ownership in non-core or lower-risk areas. Teams managing developer outreach and LinkedIn's post-acquisition integration were given broad autonomy.

For example, LinkedIn CEO Jeff Weiner continued to operate with independence under Microsoft's umbrella, retaining his team and approach, because Nadella trusted the capability and the stakes were more evolutionary than existential.

Leadership Role: Coach & Observer

Nadella provided high-level guidance but avoided interference, focusing his energy where leadership leverage was most needed.

Takeaway

Leadership shifts based on context: Nadella didn't impose a static leadership style; he adapted his ownership based on team capability and outcome criticality.

Trust as a strategic lever: Instead of hoarding control, Nadella used trust to amplify ownership across the organisation.

The journey from crisis to autonomy: Effective leaders begin by owning responsibility when no one else can, and gradually distribute ownership when others are ready.

This case demonstrates that leadership maturity lies not in doing everything, but in knowing what must be done by you, and what must grow through others.

Case Study 2: Narayana Health – Dr. Devi Shetty's Shift from Surgeon to System Builder

Context

Founded in 2000 by cardiac surgeon Dr. Devi Shetty, Narayana Health began with a bold vision to make world-class healthcare affordable for all. At inception, the mission was both critical (saving lives, building credibility) and the team was relatively low in maturity - a typical Quadrant 1: Direct Ownership scenario.

Phase 1: Direct Ownership – Building Credibility Through Personal Involvement

Dr. Shetty, a renowned heart surgeon, personally led surgeries, supervised operations, and made executive decisions. In the early days, he was the face, the force, and the fallback for everything, ranging from patient care protocols to business development.

Leadership Role: Steward & Executor

The hospital's success relied heavily on his hands-on involvement. Direct ownership was essential to build trust in a high-stakes domain like cardiac care.

Phase 2: Shared Ownership – Scaling Through Process and Talent

As Narayana Health expanded from one hospital in Bengaluru to a nationwide network, Dr. Shetty began sharing ownership with a carefully groomed leadership team. Clinical protocols were codified, IT systems standardised, and unit heads were empowered to run regional hospitals.

For instance, Chief Operating Officers of various centres were given autonomy over daily decisions, while corporate monitored quality and alignment with the broader vision.

Leadership Role: Facilitator & Enabler

While the mission (affordable healthcare at scale) remained critical, the growing capability of regional leaders enabled him to delegate and scale effectively.

Phase 3: Delegated Ownership – Technology, Telemedicine, and Beyond

Dr. Shetty deliberately delegated ownership of emerging frontiers such as telemedicine, medical tech integration, and insurance innovation to younger professionals and entrepreneurial teams within the organisation.

The team behind *Yeshashvini*, the pioneering rural health insurance scheme, operated semi-independently, with Dr. Shetty providing vision but not micro-level control.

Leadership Role: Coach & Observer

These were important but lower-risk initiatives. Delegating gave rise to innovation while allowing Dr. Shetty to focus on future-facing strategy and policy advocacy.

Takeaway

From genius to generative leadership: Dr. Shetty moved from being the best individual contributor to the architect of a self-sustaining system.

Empowerment with scaffolding: Delegation was not abandonment; it came with support structures like process manuals, regular audits, and cultural alignment.

Legacy through distribution: By distributing ownership, Narayana Health became scalable and resilient beyond its founder.

Final Reflection

Both Satya Nadella and Dr. Devi Shetty showcase an advanced understanding of ownership.

They knew that owning less of the 'how' eventually allowed them to own more of the 'why' and 'where to next.'

This is the subtle superpower of evolved leadership, the ability to remain in charge without always being in control.

CHAPTER 4

The Unaccountability Economy

Some industries thrive on the ability to shift, obscure, or dilute responsibility. Legal loopholes, bureaucratic processes, and corporate shielding create an environment where no single entity bears full accountability. This systemic responsibility dodging has broad implications for ethics, trust, and governance. The real challenge for leaders in such an environment is to redefine success, not as avoiding accountability, but as having the strength to uphold integrity even when the system is built to blur it.

4.1 Investigating Entire Industries Built on Shifting Responsibility

(Legal loopholes, corporate shielding, bureaucracy)

Behind the polished facades of skyscrapers, beyond glossy marketing campaigns and neatly packaged disclaimers, lies a thriving, systemic phenomenon, an entire economy built not on delivering accountability, but on evading it.

Welcome to the Unaccountability Economy. This is a place where responsibility isn't shouldered but shuffled, where the buck never stops. It simply disappears into a labyrinth of ambiguity. In this sector, the most valued skill is not ownership, but the art of disowning consequence - legally, structurally, and emotionally.

4.1.1   Legal Loopholes: Precision Without Conscience

The legal world is designed to uphold justice, but paradoxically, some of its finest minds are employed not to establish truth, but to insulate their clients from it. When lawyers and consultants exploit technicalities to help corporations avoid taxes, liabilities, or ethical obligations, they weaponise the law not as a shield for the innocent but as a smokescreen for the evasive.

Tax havens, transfer pricing schemes, offshore accounts; these aren't merely financial instruments; they are escape routes. Entire industries exist to create an illusion of compliance while subverting its essence. The question is not whether the action is right, but whether it can be justified legally, if not morally.

The paradox is chilling: The more complex the law becomes, the easier it is to hide within it.

4.1.2   Corporate Shielding: The Anatomy of Detached Entities

Limited liability was invented as a tool to encourage enterprise and risk-taking. But in the unaccountability economy, it has evolved into a fortress of detachment. Leaders make reckless decisions for short-term profits, and when fallout ensues, the entity, not the individuals, is held to account. Fines are paid, but no one is fired. Profits remain private; losses are socialised.

This structure incentivises what may be termed 'strategic irresponsibility', a model in which executives act boldly, knowing that their personal risk is minimal, while their upside is maximised.

Holding companies, subsidiaries, and shell corporations further fragment responsibility. When damage is done, whether it's an oil spill, a data breach, or financial fraud, the blame is scattered like dust in the wind. By the time investigators trace accountability, the original actors have long moved on or disappeared behind another layer of insulation.

It's the corporate version of plausible deniability, engineered at scale.

4.1.3 Bureaucracy: The Disappearance of the Individual

If legal loopholes and corporate shielding externalise responsibility, bureaucracy internalises its evasion. Here, it is not the absence of people, but the absence of personal clarity, that causes accountability to vanish.

In bureaucracies, tasks are divided, and decision-making is diffused. Every action is traceable to a committee, a policy, or a process, never a person. When failures occur, the answer is almost always some variation of 'the system didn't work', or worse, 'we followed the process.'

Paradoxically, the very processes that were designed to ensure diligence end up becoming alibis for inaction. 'Following the rules' becomes more important than doing what is right. Individuals, even well-meaning ones, are conditioned to prioritise compliance over conscience.

In such an environment, accountability is not merely avoided; it becomes structurally impossible.

4.1.4 The Culture of Disassociation

At the heart of this unaccountability economy is a culture of disassociation. The language gives it away. Phrases like 'mistakes were made', 'policies were violated', and 'there was a breach' are all passive, all stripped of agency. No names. No ownership. No soul.

The tragic irony is that in industries built to serve, such as finance, healthcare, education, governance, responsibility is most absent where it is most needed. People become customers, cases, statistics. Metrics replace meaning. And in the pursuit of efficiency, humanity is quietly amputated.

4.1.5   A Question of Design, Not Decay

This is not a temporary lapse of ethics. It is a design feature, not a bug. Entire industries, like consulting, lobbying, compliance, and even public relations, have been built to manage perception rather than performance, appearance rather than integrity.

We have created systems that reward evasive brilliance more than courageous leadership.

The paradox is thus: the more advanced our systems of control and oversight become, the easier it becomes to hide within them.

4.1.6   Case Studies: The Art of Structured Irresponsibility

1. Enron – Legal Complexity as Camouflage

At the height of its success, Enron was the darling of Wall Street, a symbol of innovation and bold capitalism. Beneath the surface, however, Enron was orchestrating a financial illusion powered by Special Purpose Entities (SPEs), off-balance-sheet arrangements, and accounting wizardry.

The company shifted debt into these SPEs to make its financials look healthier than they were. Executives claimed ignorance, auditors turned a blind eye, and regulators were late to react. The result? Investors lost billions, employees lost pensions, and Arthur Andersen, once a respected audit firm, collapsed.

But here's the catch. Many of the transactions were technically legal. The law had been used not to reveal truth, but to obscure it.

Lesson: When complexity becomes a weapon, truth becomes collateral damage.

2. Bhopal Gas Tragedy – Corporate Shielding at Its Worst

In 1984, a toxic gas leak from a pesticide plant owned by Union Carbide India Limited (UCIL) killed thousands and injured over half a million people in Bhopal, India. Union Carbide Corporation (UCC), the American parent company, denied full liability, citing UCIL's operational independence.

Legal and jurisdictional shielding tactics allowed UCC to evade full reparations. Dow Chemical, which acquired UCC later, further distanced itself from the disaster, claiming no legal responsibility for UCC's past liabilities.

Despite years of court cases and protests, the victims never received justice proportional to the damage inflicted.

Lesson: The architecture of corporate separation enables moral abandonment.

3. The 2008 Financial Crisis – Bureaucratic Evasion and Systemic Irresponsibility

In the run-up to the 2008 global financial crisis, major banks and financial institutions knowingly sold mortgage-backed securities filled with high-risk loans. Rating agencies gave them triple-A ratings. Regulators failed to intervene. When the house of cards collapsed, the fallout was catastrophic.

Billions were wiped out. Homes were foreclosed. Governments had to bail out institutions deemed 'too big to fail'.

Yet, remarkably few individuals were held criminally accountable. Executives cited systemic failures, algorithmic errors, or lack of foresight. Complex bureaucracy and corporate opacity provided the perfect cover.

Lesson: When everyone is responsible, no one is accountable.

4. Cambridge Analytica – Consent Without Understanding

Cambridge Analytica harvested data from over 80 million Facebook profiles to manipulate voter behaviour during elections, including Brexit and the 2016 U.S. Presidential race. Though users had technically 'consented', the design of the platform exploited vague permissions and opaque privacy policies.

Facebook's response was classic deflection: *'We didn't break the law.'* The company cooperated with investigations, but its leadership deflected personal blame.

Lesson: Consent is meaningless when users don't understand what they're consenting to, and platforms know it.

5. Sahara Group – The Shell Game of Compliance

For years, the Sahara India Pariwar amassed vast sums from small investors, especially in rural and semi-urban India, through optionally fully convertible debentures. The Securities and Exchange Board of India (SEBI) found these instruments to be illegal public offerings.

Even after a Supreme Court ruling directing Sahara to refund over ₹24,000 crore to investors, the group's legal battles, delays, and complex corporate structuring stalled restitution.

Sahara's top leadership was briefly jailed but largely retained operational control. Many investors remain uncompensated even today.

Lesson: When the legal system moves at the pace of privilege, justice becomes a performance, not a promise.

6. PNB-Nirav Modi Scam – Fragile Systems, Dispersed Blame

In one of the largest banking scams in India's history, jeweller Nirav Modi and associates defrauded Punjab National Bank (PNB) of over ₹13,000 crore using fraudulent Letters of Undertaking (LoUs), undetected for years.

The process exploited back-door access in banking systems and relied on employees who bypassed internal checks. Yet, the scale of the fraud suggests systemic negligence, if not silent collusion.

Top PNB management distanced themselves, blaming rogue employees and system vulnerabilities. Nirav Modi fled the country, and extradition proceedings are still ongoing.

Lesson: In rigid hierarchies, accountability rarely flows upward.

7. Public Sector Projects – The Bureaucratic Fog

Projects such as Commonwealth Games 2010 have often been riddled with cost overruns, inefficiencies, and lack of measurable outcomes. Yet, accountability is almost always dispersed.

Reports from CAG (Comptroller and Auditor General) highlight serious irregularities. But bureaucrats cite process fidelity, ministers pass the buck to contractors, and contractors blame procedural delays. By the time audits are published, the personnel have changed, and the institutional memory resets.

Lesson: Bureaucracies master the art of accountability without ownership.

Summary

These case studies are not isolated failures - they form a pattern of structured evasion, a sophisticated choreography of denial where legal finesse, corporate shielding, and bureaucratic fragmentation work in concert to obscure truth and diffuse responsibility.

This is the real face of the Unaccountability Economy, not a villain with a smoking gun, but a system engineered to let individuals and institutions walk away from wreckage with clean hands and a clear conscience.

In the Indian context, this phenomenon takes a sharper shape; accountability is often inversely proportional to power. Systems are not designed to expose failure but to absorb and outlive it. Public memory is short. Legal proceedings are protracted. And administrative clarity is elusive by design.

What emerges is not disorder but an engineered fog, a deliberate ambiguity that lets institutional failure persist without consequence. The moral cost? A society where responsibility becomes a slogan, not a standard.

4.2 Profitability of Unaccountability – How Systems Reward Evasion Over Integrity

4.2.1 Case Studies

Case 1

In 2013, the National Spot Exchange Limited (NSEL), once a flourishing commodities trading platform in India, collapsed in a ₹5,600 crore scam involving a fake trading ring. The scam was a web of deceit, with brokers and operators selling non-existent goods, while auditors and regulators turned a blind eye. Traders lost everything, but what stands out most is the delayed, diluted accountability; the regulators spent years wrangling over jurisdiction, and the promoters walked free with their wealth.

This is not an isolated instance. Unaccountability is not just a moral lapse. It is an economic model, a silent engine of advantage for those who know how to manipulate it. For those who understand its architecture, evasion is not a desperate act; it is a strategy. One that, ironically, the system incentivises.

From inflated valuations to regulatory arbitrage, from cosmetic compliance to plausible deniability, every layer of modern systems, corporate, bureaucratic, even political, often sends a singular message: *It pays to not be caught, and even more to not be responsible.*

Case 2

In 2018, the Punjab National Bank fraud, orchestrated by Nirav Modi and Mehul Choksi, shook the Indian banking system. Over ₹13,000 crore siphoned off through fake Letters of Undertaking, unchecked for years. The astonishing part? Not just the scale of fraud, but the ease with which internal checks were bypassed, and the time it took for the system to even detect it. Even after discovery, the accountability trail was murky. Senior executives claimed ignorance. Auditors pointed to procedural loopholes. Regulatory bodies launched investigations that were slow, scattered, and inconclusive.

While the banks bled, the system stayed intact. Promotions resumed. Elections moved on. Institutions survived; yet ownership remained elusive.

This case is not an outlier. It exemplifies a larger truth: *Unaccountability is not just a lapse. It is a business model. A design feature.* For those who understand its architecture, evading responsibility is not an exception; it is a strategy. And the system, knowingly or unknowingly, rewards it.

4.2.2   The Cost-Benefit Analysis of Evasion

At the heart of this phenomenon lies a distorted calculus. Integrity is expensive. It requires investment in transparency, rigorous processes, slower decision-making, and occasionally sacrificing short-term profits. Evasion, on the other hand, offers high returns with diffused risk.

Consider the case of environmental clearances in India. Companies that delay or avoid compliance may face penalties eventually, but only after years of litigation. Meanwhile, they continue to profit. The penalty becomes a calculated cost of doing business, not a deterrent.

Or take tax evasion versus tax planning. The more intricate the scheme, the harder it is to pin down responsibility. The reward? Lower tax liability. The risk? Often minimal, thanks to under-staffed enforcement, weak prosecution, and negotiated settlements.

4.2.3   The Moral Arbitrage

This system creates what might be called 'moral arbitrage', a gap between what is ethically right and what is legally enforceable. Those with the resources and knowledge to exploit this gap build empires on the thin ice of selective compliance.

In India, real estate developers routinely launch projects without full approvals, confident that either regulators will look the other way or that post-facto regularisation will be negotiated. Buyers suffer. Officials plead helplessness. Developers walk away with profits.

Here, it's not about breaking the law; it's about bending it so gracefully that no one can tell where integrity ended and impunity began.

4.2.4   Regulatory Theatre and the Myth of Oversight

Most systems maintain a performance of regulation rather than the practice of it. Audits, compliance reports, internal committees; all create the illusion of oversight. But real accountability is often stage-managed.

In sectors like banking or public procurement, procedural adherence often replaces outcome responsibility. As long as the paperwork is in order, the result, no matter how wasteful or damaging, is insulated from consequence.

This transforms systems into process-driven vaults of irresponsibility; you can hide behind protocols even when the collapse is visible.

4.2.5   The Normalisation of Ethical Compromise

In such an environment, integrity becomes the anomaly. Whistleblowers are not heroes; they are threats to equilibrium. Transparent operators are edged out by those who play the grey zones more efficiently.

Over time, this creates cultural erosion. Not because people are inherently unethical, but because the system communicates clearly that integrity is bad for business. The faster you learn to look the other way, the higher you rise.

Unaccountability is not just permitted; it is rewarded with promotion, profit, and power.

4.2.6   Systemic Amnesia and the Cycles of Evasion

Once an incident passes the public eye, systems conveniently forget. Executives re-emerge in new roles. Companies rebrand. Bureaucrats retire or are transferred. Politicians deny knowledge. Media moves on.

This amnesia is not accidental; it is engineered by slow investigations, fragmented responsibility, and institutional fatigue. The message is clear: *time heals all scandals.*

4.2.7   The Inversion of Virtue and Value

In this paradox, virtue carries a cost, while evasion delivers return on investment. This is the most dangerous feature of the Unaccountability Economy, not just that evasion happens, but that it thrives.

When systems reward those who play the game without honouring its principles, integrity becomes not just rare, but irrational. And when that inversion becomes normal, we don't just lose accountability; we lose the very aspiration to own with pride. We inherit power without stewardship, and success without soul.

4.2.8   The Cultural Cost of Systemic Evasion

But the profitability of unaccountability doesn't just distort economics; it reprogrammes the moral software of society.

When systems consistently reward evasion, it begins to shape more than incentives; it begins to shape values. Policymakers learn to draft rules with wiggle room, not enforcement. Corporate leaders design controls that check boxes, not behaviour. Citizens internalise the message that it is safer to conform silently than to stand responsibly.

This slow drift births a culture of anticipatory abdication. Decisions are made not to solve, but to shift. Policies are framed not to protect, but to pre-empt blame. The end result is a society where ownership is feared, and accountability is seen as a liability.

Even personal ethics are affected. Young professionals learn early that asking tough questions invites isolation. Bureaucrats master the art of looking busy while doing little. Entrepreneurs hedge values against loopholes. What begins as a survival tactic becomes a way of life, a default orientation of avoidance.

The paradox is complete: the more unaccountability is normalised, the less society remembers how to take responsibility at all.

4.3   Is Absolute Responsibility a Myth in a World of Diffused Ownership?

In the idealised corridors of leadership theory and organisational design, responsibility is often portrayed as a clear-cut line, a chain of command, a structure of accountability, a ledger of ownership. But in the real world, where complexity breeds collaboration, and where roles, systems, and stakeholders overlap, the idea of absolute responsibility begins to appear not just rare, but illusory.

4.3.1   The Modern Mosaic of Shared Decisions

Today's institutions operate in ecosystems, not silos. Decisions are taken by cross-functional entities, executed across multiple actors, and influenced by regulators, outsourced agencies, technical partners, media narratives, and political considerations. When a disaster strikes, the question of "Who is responsible?" often invites a chorus of technicalities and deflections, rather than a confession of accountability.

4.3.2   Case Study

The Morbi Bridge Collapse (Gujarat, 2022)

On October 30, 2022, the suspension bridge over the Machchhu River in Morbi, Gujarat, collapsed just four days after being reopened to the public following renovations. Over 130 lives were lost, many of them children and families who had come to enjoy the festive weekend. The public outcry was immediate. But so was the diffusion of responsibility.

The Municipal authorities claimed that they had not given final approval for reopening.

The private contractor (Oreva Group) claimed they had completed structural renovations and that the bridge was reopened under public pressure.

Regulatory oversight bodies were either silent or evasive about inspection protocols.

Police investigations pointed to mechanical failures and crowd overcapacity, but the root of the systemic failure remained vague.

The state administration distanced itself by pointing to third-party contracts and procedural compliance.

In the aftermath, several junior staff and technicians were arrested. But the larger web of oversight, procurement terms, contractor qualifications, safety audits, and civic accountability remained untouched in public discourse. There was public tragedy, but no singular public accountability.

Everyone had a justification. No one took ownership.

This incident did not arise from malice, but from complacency, procedural opacity, and a disjointed chain of command. It exposed the illusion of absolute responsibility in a system where governance, execution, and inspection were split across disjointed domains. Each had its own slice of plausible deniability.

4.3.3   The Paradox of Everyone and No One

This is the paradox of diffused ownership: when everyone shares responsibility, it often feels like no one owns it. Tasks are distributed; outcomes are aggregated. Failures, especially, are camouflaged within this diffusion. *"We did what we were supposed to,"* says every party. And they may be right, technically. But the sum of all compliant parts can still result in fatal failure.

The myth of absolute responsibility persists because it comforts us; we want to pinpoint failure, assign blame, and move on. But systems thinking reveals a harsher truth: *responsibility in complex structures isn't clear-cut. It is spread out, layered, and often hidden by administrative convenience.*

4.3.4   Can Responsibility Be Reconstructed?

Rather than lament the erosion of absolute responsibility, modern leadership must ask: *Can we redesign accountability in systems where ownership is naturally distributed?*

The answer lies in constructive interdependence; where each stakeholder understands the implications of their action or inaction, and systems are built not to transfer blame, but to build clarity. This requires:

Transparent audit trails: Not just compliance checklists, but clarity on "who knew what, when, and why."

Layered responsibility matrices: Going beyond roles on paper to define accountability in operational, ethical, and public dimensions.

Consequential collaboration: Creating structures where collective action leads to collective responsibility, not isolated scapegoating.

4.3.5   Responsibility as a Lived Ethic, Not a Legal Clause

Ultimately, the notion of 'absolute responsibility' may be more about moral courage than managerial assignment. In the absence of legal finality, what remains is personal leadership, the ability to say, *"Even if this wasn't directly my doing, I am still accountable for the impact."*

Diffused ownership is a functional reality. But that need not translate into ethical anonymity. Responsibility may not be absolute, but it must be felt. And it must be seen.

4.3.6   A Moral Insight: Leadership Rooted in Dharm, Not Delegation

In a world where accountability is scattered and responsibility diluted, true leadership must rise beyond contractual obligation and procedural defense. It must be anchored in Dharm - the ethical compass that transcends roles and rules.

In the Mahabharat, when the Pandavs lost everything in the dice game, Yudhishthir could have easily blamed Shakuni's deceit or Duryodhan's arrogance. Yet he held himself accountable, not because he was solely to blame, but because he saw himself as answerable to a higher ideal of leadership. His regret was not just personal; it was moral. That is the essence of value-based ownership.

Modern leaders must similarly adopt a shift, moving from positional authority to moral responsibility. They must cultivate:

Internal accountability: Holding themselves answerable not just for outcomes, but for intentions and omissions.

Ethical foresight: Anticipating how today's delegation can become tomorrow's denial.

Conscious stewardship: Knowing that leadership is not about owning credit, but absorbing consequence.

Such leadership does not wait for crises to expose the cracks. It operates in the silent zones, where paperwork ends but conscience begins. It takes ownership not because the contract demands it, but because character commands it.

In the Unaccountability Economy, value-based leaders are those rare individuals who still choose to say: *"It was my responsibility. I will make it right."*

4.4   The Ownership Compass: Navigating Responsibility in a Fragmented World

When absolute responsibility is no longer realistic, and blame is easily passed along the corridors of complexity, what can guide a leader? The answer is not more control, but better orientation. Like a sailor without a clear shoreline, the modern leader needs a compass, not to pinpoint blame, but to anchor direction.

4.4.1   The Ownership Compass

The Ownership Compass is not a map, it's a mindset. It helps leaders navigate ambiguity, diffuse authority, and moral complexity by aligning them to four cardinal anchors of responsible leadership:

1. North – Moral Clarity (Why am I truly accountable?)

This is the ethical north star. Beyond roles and rules, leaders must ask:

What is the right thing to do, and why must I own it, even if I didn't cause it?

Moral clarity helps you take proactive ownership in grey areas: *when no one is watching, and no line on the org chart says it's your job. It is rooted in Dharm, not just documentation.*

2. East – Systemic Awareness (What is the real structure of responsibility?)

Before taking or assigning responsibility, understand the ecosystem:

Who are the silent stakeholders?

What dependencies exist?

Where does information flow stop?

Systemic awareness prevents both naive blame and blind self-sacrifice. It respects complexity while resisting its use as a cover for inaction.

3. South – Courageous Accountability (Will I stand up when others step back?)

This is the test of character. When things go wrong, people hide behind processes, teams, and consultants. Courageous accountability means saying:

"This may not be entirely my fault, but it is my watch. I will respond."

Such leaders inspire trust not because they never fail, but because they never flee from the fallout.

4. West – Constructive Action (What will I do to make it better?)

Ownership is not just confession; it is correction. Leaders who stop at admission are moral narrators. Those who take corrective, healing, or preventive action are true stewards. Constructive action means:

Learning from failure.

Reforming systems.

Elevating the standard for future decisions.

It moves responsibility from rhetoric to repair.

<u>**Using the Compass in Practice**</u>

Whenever you're in a situation where responsibility is unclear or contested, pause and ask:

North: What is the right thing to do, even if inconvenient?

East: Do I fully understand how the system contributed to this?

South: Am I willing to be seen taking ownership, even if I'm not solely responsible?

West: What action can I take today to make this right or prevent recurrence?

This compass turns good intent into wise leadership. It helps you navigate not just crises, but complexity; where ethical maps are missing, but moral direction is vital.

4.4.2 Case Study: Restoring Trust After the Chennai Floods – A Tale of Constructive Ownership

Context

In December 2015, Chennai experienced catastrophic flooding due to record-breaking rainfall. While the deluge was triggered by natural forces, the scale of devastation, hundreds dead, thousands displaced, and urban paralysis, was largely man-made. Investigations revealed:

Poor drainage infrastructure.

Encroachments on water bodies.

Ill-planned urbanisation.

Delayed warning and poor coordination among civic bodies.

Responsibility was everywhere. And nowhere.

As agencies scrambled to shift blame, from municipal authorities to the state government, from builders to weather departments, one public servant, IAS officer Shri J. Radhakrishnan, then Commissioner of Relief and Rehabilitation, became a quiet exemplar of value-based leadership.

He didn't cause the floods. But he took ownership of the response.

Applying the Ownership Compass

North – Moral Clarity: Rather than deflect responsibility onto natural forces or historical decisions, Radhakrishnan focused on a simple question: *What is the right thing to do now for the people who are suffering?*

He saw his role not as an administrator defending legacy errors, but as a human being entrusted with alleviating pain. His clarity was rooted in service, not survival.

"People were wading through chest-deep water. The system was slow. We needed urgency, not bureaucracy." – J. Radhakrishnan

East – Systemic Awareness: He recognised that floods were a result of systemic failure. So instead of patchwork responses, he initiated cross-agency coordination:

Mobilised district officials, health workers, and volunteers under one command.

Partnered with NGOs, corporates, and citizen groups.

Ordered real-time data sharing between departments to track rescue operations and medical needs.

He didn't simplify the problem. He understood the layers, and wove them into a coherent response.

South – Courageous Accountability: While others feared media backlash and political criticism, Radhakrishnan made field visits in flooded areas, took public questions, and gave daily press briefings. He stood visible; not to claim success, but to absorb anger, guide citizens, and course-correct fast.

He shielded junior officers from blame and empowered them to take decisions on the ground without red tape.

"Don't wait for orders. If it helps people, do it and report later." – His message to field officers

West – Constructive Action: He didn't just restore roads and electricity. He launched systemic initiatives post-floods:

Early warning systems and WhatsApp-based disaster alerts.

Community-based disaster response training.

Rapid outbreak control mechanisms (no major epidemics were reported despite the floods).

His actions set a benchmark for disaster governance, not just in Tamil Nadu, but nationally.

The Takeaway: When Systems Fail, Leaders Must Not

J. Radhakrishnan's leadership didn't come from titles; it came from moral intent and decisive action. In a fractured system where everyone was technically right but morally absent, he used the Ownership Compass to step up:

Moral Clarity over blame.

Systemic Awareness over isolation.

Courageous Accountability over deflection.

Constructive Action over reactive firefighting.

His example proves: *even in the Unaccountability Economy, responsibility can be reclaimed, not by waiting for someone else to own it, but by choosing to own what matters.*

4.4.3   Action Guide: Bringing the Ownership Compass to Life in Your Organisation

In today's complex and interconnected organisations, responsibility often dissolves into departmental silos, delayed decisions, and defensive posturing. Leaders who wish to build a culture of value-based ownership must operationalise the Ownership Compass, turning its four directions into daily practices.

Here's how to get started:

1. North – Moral Clarity: Anchor Decisions in Purpose

Define a leadership charter

Write a personal leadership manifesto or team charter that clearly outlines why you lead, not just what you manage.

Ask the right questions

In moments of uncertainty, ask:

"If no one else responds, will I?"

"What is the right thing to do, even if it's not popular or officially required?"

Reward integrity, not just output

Publicly recognise team members who demonstrate moral courage, especially when they take a stand for what's right, even at personal risk.

2. East – Systemic Awareness: See the Bigger Picture

Map responsibility chains

Before launching a project, map the real ecosystem of stakeholders, not just by org chart, but by influence and impact.

Conduct a 'blame delay' analysis

In every post-mortem or debrief, identify moments when the team waited for someone else to act. Uncover where responsibility was technically absent but morally present.

Promote cross-functional empathy

Host 'walk-a-mile' sessions where departments briefly shadow each other's roles. This builds understanding of how decisions affect the whole system.

3. South – Courageous Accountability: Step Up, Visibly

Model vulnerability

In times of failure, openly say: *"I take responsibility for this. Here's what we learned. Here's how we'll make it better."* This gives others psychological permission to do the same.

Empower judgment on the ground

Encourage your teams: *"If it aligns with our values, act. We'll support you even if you stumble."* Make it safe to be bold for the right reasons.

Hold open forums during crises

Rather than avoiding tough conversations, facilitate them. Let teams express concern, suggest fixes, and see you stand accountable.

4. West – Constructive Action: Own the Solution

Prioritise course correction over control

When things go wrong, focus on: *"How do we fix this fast and learn from it?"* instead of *"Who messed up and why?"*

Institutionalise learnings

After a setback or a win, update SOPs, training, or workflows. Show that ownership leads to tangible improvements, not just applause.

Create 'responsibility labs'

Run simulations or case scenarios where teams must respond to ambiguous problems without clear roles. Reflect together on who stepped up, and why.

Bringing It All Together

Ownership isn't an announcement. It's a muscle, built through repetition, reflection, and reinforcement. Use this mini-checklist:

Direction	Key Question	Leader's Practice
North (Clarity)	Am I doing what's right, or what's easy?	Pause to align actions with values
East (System)	Do I understand the whole impact chain?	Map stakeholders before acting
South (Courage)	Will I stand up even when it's uncomfortable?	Take visible responsibility
West (Action)	Am I fixing the issue or just fixing the blame?	Lead solutions and embed the learning

4.4.4   Final Word: Leadership That Reclaims the Centre

In the Unaccountability Economy, the leaders who stand out are not those who never err, but those who never abandon the moral centre of gravity.

With the Ownership Compass, you won't control every outcome. But you'll always know which way is true north.

4.5   *The Blame Trap: When Accountability is Weaponised*

Responsibility becomes toxic when it's used not to fix problems, but to fix people.

"It was not my fault."

"They didn't follow the process."

"I was only doing what I was told."

These aren't just post-failure rationalisations. They are survival instincts, symptoms of an organisational culture where accountability has morphed into blame. When accountability is weaponised, responsibility stops being a shared value and becomes a tool for scapegoating.

In such environments, leaders no longer seek the truth of what went wrong; they seek the target.

4.5.1   The Psychology of Blame

Blame, as a default response, often comes from the need to:

Protect image and reputation

Deflect systemic scrutiny

Avoid discomfort or consequences

Reinforce power dynamics

Ironically, the more a leader insists on 'finding the culprit', the less likely the team is to speak up, admit lapses, or collaborate on sustainable fixes.

Blame creates compliance, not commitment.

4.5.2   The Accountability–Culpability Confusion

One of the root causes of blame culture is the failure to distinguish between:

Culpability: Who caused the error?

Responsibility: Who has the ability to respond constructively?

In healthy systems, accountability looks ahead, focusing on learning, prevention, and resolution. In toxic systems, it looks backward, focusing on punishment and naming-and-shaming.

This confusion:

Destroys initiative, as people avoid taking ownership of anything uncertain.

Breeds silence, where early warnings and whistleblowers are ignored.

Leads to underperformance, where mediocrity feels safer than bold action.

4.5.3   Corporate Example: The Blame Game After a Data Breach

In 2023, a prominent Indian fintech company experienced a serious data breach, exposing sensitive customer details. In the internal post-mortem, the initial reaction from leadership was not curiosity or containment, but urgency to assign blame.

The IT team blamed the cloud provider.

The CISO blamed outdated policies.

Marketing blamed poor internal communication.

Leadership blamed a 'non-compliant' middle manager, who was eventually suspended.

However, external audits later revealed that:

The company had no unified data governance framework.

Risk registers were outdated.

Budget approvals for cybersecurity upgrades had been delayed at the top level.

By the time truth emerged, the damage was done, morale was low, reputation was hit, and trust had eroded - internally and externally. A classic case of accountability being used as a shield, not a solution.

4.5.4 From Blame to Constructive Ownership

To break free from the Blame Trap, leaders must shift from *Who do we blame?* to *What can we learn?*

Here's a three-part approach:

1. **Decouple learning from punishment:** Not every failure needs a head to roll. Build psychological safety by encouraging the surfacing of problems before they become crises.
2. **Make system failure the default hypothesis:** Ask first: *What in our system allowed this to happen?* Instead of: *Who messed up?* Usually, the issue lies in handovers, silos, assumptions, or outdated processes.
3. **Be publicly accountable, privately corrective:** Leaders should absorb responsibility in public and resolve root causes in private. This builds trust while keeping the team open to growth.

4.5.5 Insight

The Shift from Accountability as Judgement to Accountability as Ownership

True accountability isn't about punishing the past. It's about enabling a better future.

A value-based leader doesn't ask Who do I penalise?

They ask: " *What am I responsible for, whether or not I caused it?*"

This mindset shifts the conversation from fault-finding to future-building.

4.6   Creating Cultures of Shared Ownership: The Antidote to Systemic Evasion

When ownership is shared, accountability is no longer feared.

In environments where no one wants to be held responsible, blame tends to spread. The only way out is to get everyone to start taking ownership together. In an era of complex teams, distributed authority, and blurred reporting lines, what organisations need isn't more rules or reactive controls, but cultures where people voluntarily raise their hands and say:

"Even if it's not my job, I will make it my concern."

This is the heart of shared ownership. It goes beyond role descriptions and KPIs. It's one thing to be accountable because it's in your job description; it's another to take responsibility simply because you care.

4.6.1   From Individual Accountability to Collective Commitment

Traditional accountability asks: *"Who's responsible?"*

Shared ownership reframes this to: *"Who all care enough to take action?"*

This subtle shift:

Prevents failure from falling through the cracks.

Encourages co-ownership across boundaries.

Builds resilience, as more people feel empowered to intervene early.

It's not about diluting ownership, but diffusing action responsibly.

4.6.2   Case Study: A Shipyard's Shift from Blame to Belonging

In an Indian public-sector shipbuilding yard, quality lapses during final inspection were leading to embarrassing delays. The blame would always flow downward to welders, charge-hands, or junior engineers.

A newly appointed GM, instead of punishing, invited every stakeholder, production, quality, safety, design, and HR, into a joint Root Cause Discovery Forum. His message was clear:

"These aren't quality problems; they're system problems. Let's own them together."

The forum unearthed:

Design teams rarely visited the shop floor.

Safety and HR teams were unaware of production pressures.

SOPs were outdated or poorly communicated.

What changed:

Cross-functional teams co-authored new inspection checklists.

Designers participated in build reviews on site.

Weekly 'ownership rounds' included all functions.

Within months, delivery quality improved, not because accountability was enforced, but because ownership was cultivated.

4.6.3   Five Foundations of Shared Ownership Culture

To embed this ethos in your organisation, build around these principles:

1. **Clarity of Purpose:** People own what they understand. Constantly communicate why their work matters, beyond metrics.

2. **Trust Before Oversight:** Micro-management breeds compliance. Trust breeds initiative. Default to trust, and let systems correct outliers.

3. **Transparency in Process:** Open access to decisions, timelines, dependencies, and risks allows proactive engagement across silos.

4. **Courageous Conversations:** Create forums where anyone can challenge, escalate, or contribute - without fear of rank or retribution.

5. **Recognition of Invisible Contribution:** Celebrate those who stepped in when they didn't have to; especially in roles or moments that usually go unnoticed.

Final Thought: When Everyone Feels Like a Steward, No One Escapes Responsibility

Instead of relying on top-down enforcement, we need a culture where people at every level feel responsible.

When people feel like stewards, not just staff, ownership becomes a shared identity, not a forced accountability.

This shift, from me to we, is how organisations transcend the blame economy and build lasting cultures of trust, action, and impact.

4.6.4   Reflection: Reclaiming Responsibility in an Era of Escape

In a world where complexity often camouflages culpability, the instinct to sidestep ownership is both natural and dangerous. We've seen how absolute responsibility may be a myth, how blame can be weaponised, and how shared ownership offers a sustainable path forward.

Ironically, the more people involved, the easier it is for everyone to avoid responsibility. That's why it's even more important for people to intentionally take ownership in complex systems.

In navigating the unaccountability economy, leaders face a moral and strategic crossroads:

Do we preserve ourselves through plausible deniability; or elevate our culture through principled ownership?

Do we play the role of watchdogs; or that of gardeners who nurture responsibility from the soil up?

Are we just trying to make sure people follow the rules, or are we helping them actually care about what they're doing?

The answer lies not in one heroic leader taking all the weight, but in many people choosing ownership without title, power, or compulsion.

Responsibility, then, is not a role assigned, but a value assumed.

And in a truly evolved organisation, ownership is not enforced; it is inevitable.

CHAPTER 5

The Burden of Knowing Too Much

With knowledge comes responsibility. Leaders often come across information they wish they had not, such as insider insights, ethical dilemmas, or hard truths about their organisation. This phenomenon, the Cursed Insight Principle, suggests that once a leader knows something, they cannot unknow it. This creates a new layer of responsibility about how to act on what they know, when to reveal information, and how to navigate moral and strategic dilemmas. Those who ignore this burden risk damaging credibility, while those who embrace it must develop the wisdom to manage uncomfortable truths with tact and courage.

5.1　What Happens When Leaders Become Aware of Uncomfortable Truths They Wish They Didn't?

In leadership, ignorance may be bliss, but insight is obligation.

There's a moment every leader dreads. It's not when the storm hits - it's when the sky is still clear, but you suddenly realise a storm is coming. And no one else sees it yet. Or worse, they see it but pretend it isn't there.

That moment, when an uncomfortable truth stares you in the face, is heavy. It feels like holding fire in your bare hands. You weren't looking for it. You didn't ask for it. But now that you know, you can't *unknow* it. And that's where the paradox begins.

To lead is to see what others don't. But what happens when what you see is disturbing, messy, or simply not supposed to exist? A flaw in the system. A toxic undercurrent in the culture. An ethical line that's already been crossed. The numbers that look good but don't feel right. The person who shines in public but corrodes people in private.

There's no official manual for what to do in those moments.

Some leaders try to look away. They rationalise. *"Maybe I'm overthinking it." "Maybe it'll correct itself."* Others hide it under layers of meetings, spreadsheets, and strategy decks, doing whatever they can to avoid facing the discomfort. But evasion doesn't dissolve truth; it only delays the reckoning.

There's also the temptation to act too quickly. Some rush to announce, expose, or fix things without thinking through the context, whether others are ready, or whether the timing is right. The impulse to do something is strong, because knowing and doing nothing can feel like moral failure. But sometimes, hasty action can cause more harm than slow, strategic response.

Uncomfortable truths, by nature, are disorienting. They test your character more than your competence. They ask: *Can you hold what is true, even if it doesn't serve you? Even if it makes things harder?*

Some truths don't come with clean choices. Just consequences. And yet, how a leader responds to those truths can shape the soul of an organisation.

It's also lonely. That can't be overstated. The burden of knowing too much often isolates. Leaders can't always share what they know, not yet. So they carry the weight alone. And in that space of solitude, doubt creeps in: *Is it really that bad? Am I making this bigger than it is? Will anyone believe me if I speak up?*

This is where inner compass matters more than outer validation. When the applause dies down and the spotlight fades, what remains is your integrity. Your ability to look in the mirror and not flinch.

Leadership, at its rawest, isn't about being celebrated; it's about being trusted, even when trust costs you comfort. The uncomfortable truths you discover aren't curses; they're calls. Not always to immediate action, but to deeper reflection, wiser preparation, and braver decisions.

Because once you know, you carry a responsibility. Not always to fix everything, but at the very least, to not look away.

And sometimes, just that, choosing not to look away, is where the real transformation begins.

5.2 How Do Leaders Decide What to Do with Uncomfortable Truths?

5.2.1

Knowing the truth is one thing. Deciding what to do with it is another.

Leaders are not just decision-makers. They are meaning-makers. When faced with uncomfortable truths that challenge the status quo, threaten reputations, or expose deep flaws in systems or people, leaders must do more than simply react. They must interpret. They must weigh not only what is right, but also what is wise. And sometimes, what is right and what is wise don't immediately agree.

This is the quiet battlefield within.

At first, there's the emotional storm. Anger, disappointment, fear. Maybe even guilt: *How did I miss this? Was I complicit by not seeing it sooner?* But emotion can't be the compass. It can alert, but it can't steer.

So the leader must pause and ask a question that rarely comes with clean answers:

"Now that I know this, what am I responsible for?"

The answer depends on many things:

The nature of the truth (Is it systemic? Personal? Ethical? Operational?)

The timing (Is the organisation ready to hear it? Can it act on it?)

The impact (Will acting now cause unintended harm? Will delay make things worse?)

And most painfully, the cost (To careers. To morale. To trust. Sometimes, even to the leader's own standing.)

This is why leadership is rarely heroic in the cinematic sense. It's often slow, unglamorous, and filled with decisions that won't be fully understood until much later, if ever.

Sometimes, the decision is to act quietly. Behind the scenes. To protect the organisation without igniting panic. Other times, it means confronting things openly. Naming the truth, even when it's unwelcome, even when it disturbs the comfort of those around you.

And then there are moments when the hardest decision is to wait. Not out of fear, but out of care. To create the right conditions where the truth can be received, processed, and transformed into something constructive.

There is a subtle skill at work here called discernment. Not just knowing what is true, but knowing when and how to move with that truth. It is the art of balancing courage with patience, and action with understanding.

The truth is, no leader gets it perfectly right.

Sometimes they move too fast and cause shockwaves. Sometimes they wait too long and lose trust. But what defines great leadership is not infallibility; it's intent. The commitment to act in the best long-term interest of people and purpose, even when the road is unclear.

In the end, truth doesn't just demand action; it demands alignment. With values. With conscience. With the very reason one chose to lead in the first place.

Because when a leader knows a difficult truth, they are no longer just leading a team or a company.

They are leading themselves.

5.2.2   Exemplar: Dr. E. Sreedharan and the Delhi Metro – Leading Through Difficult Truths

In the late 1990s, when the Delhi Metro project was in its infancy, India had a history of delayed infrastructure projects plagued by cost overruns, corruption, and bureaucratic lethargy. Expectations were low. The public had seen promises made, broken, and forgotten. The uncomfortable truth? People didn't really believe a clean, timely, and efficient metro system could be built in India. Not in Delhi. Not with this system.

When Dr. E. Sreedharan was appointed as the Managing Director of the Delhi Metro Rail Corporation (DMRC), he stepped into this climate of cynicism. Early on, he noticed something most people wouldn't say out loud. There was a deep-rooted culture of compromise, with political interference, little accountability, and a casual attitude toward delays and rising costs.

It would have been easy, even expected, for him to 'play along'. To shrug and say, *"This is how the system works."* That would have been the safe thing to do.

But here's where his leadership stood apart. Dr. Sreedharan recognised the uncomfortable truths, and chose not to normalise them. Instead, he set boundaries. He demanded autonomy from political interference. He instituted strict timelines and held people accountable. He insulated the project from the 'usual ways' of doing things.

This wasn't just about engineering. It was moral leadership.

He saw the cracks in the system, and chose not to look away. But rather than loudly condemning the system, he quietly built an alternative. And he built it within the system. That was the masterstroke.

He often had to make tough decisions, like removing contractors, standing up to officials, and refusing to change timelines just to make things easier. He carried truths that others didn't want to hear: that corruption had to be actively kept out, that deadlines were sacred, and that public projects could be world-class if the leadership refused to lower the bar.

The Delhi Metro was finished on time, stayed within budget, and met global standards. In the world of Indian infrastructure, that felt almost like a miracle.

But the deeper success lay in what it proved: Uncomfortable truths, when held with integrity and acted upon with quiet resolve, can become turning points, not just for a project, but for an entire belief system.

Dr. Sreedharan's story isn't one of defiance. It's one of disciplined responsibility. He didn't just know the truth; he acted on it, wisely, consistently, and with extraordinary self-restraint.

And in doing so, he redefined what leadership could look like.

5.2.3 The Silent Legacy: When Leaders Choose Truth Over Comfort

When a leader comes face-to-face with an uncomfortable truth, no one claps. There's no fanfare. No headlines. Often, not even recognition. The moment is quiet, even lonely. But the decision that follows can echo far beyond that silence.

Because the legacy of such leadership is rarely visible in the moment. It doesn't come from big speeches or dramatic reforms. It comes from the cumulative power of quiet courage. From the unwavering decision to choose what is right, even when it's inconvenient. From holding the line when no one else is watching.

Leaders like Dr. E. Sreedharan didn't just build physical infrastructure. They rebuilt belief. In integrity, in systems, in what's possible. They created a new reference point.

And that's the true legacy: when future leaders, standing at their own crossroads, recall not just what was built, but how it was built. With clarity. With conscience. Without compromise.

This is what separates performative leadership from transformative leadership.

Transformative leaders don't just solve problems. They reshape expectations. They show us that excellence without excuses is possible. That systems can be cleaned. That the truth, even when it burdens, can be carried with dignity, and can light the path forward.

The paradox of inescapable ownership is this: Once you know, you're changed. And once you act from that knowing, so is everyone around you.

And perhaps the most powerful legacies are not the ones etched in stone, but the ones quietly engraved into the minds and hearts of those who watched you not look away.

5.3   *The Weight of Information Asymmetry - How Responsibility Increases with Knowledge*

5.3.1

There's a quiet, unspoken burden that accompanies those who know more. Not just knowledge in the academic sense, but insight, foresight, and context. In leadership, in relationships, in institutions; it is rarely a level playing field of information. Some know more than others, and with that imbalance comes a subtle but serious shift in responsibility.

This is the paradox of information asymmetry: the more you understand, the less you can pretend you don't. And the moment you know, you are no longer just a participant; you become, in some measure, accountable.

A junior officer may carry out orders, believing in the structure above. A senior leader, privy to systemic cracks, future risks, or ethical dilemmas, cannot plead ignorance. And when they do, the system pays a price. With knowledge comes a silent contract; you must now either act on it, guard it wisely, or bear the cost of not doing so.

What makes this asymmetry burdensome is not just the weight of action; it's also the emotional toll of awareness. Knowing that others are unaware. Knowing that choices you make, even in silence or delay, ripple through people who don't see the full picture. It creates an ethical dilemma: *Should you speak up or wait? Should you protect the system or disrupt it to correct it?*

5.3.2   Examples

The Bhopal Gas Tragedy of 1984

When the gas leak occurred at the Union Carbide India Limited (UCIL) plant, thousands of lives were devastated. But what's more haunting is that the signs were known. Multiple employees had flagged safety concerns. Internal reports existed. Technical personnel had knowledge about maintenance shortcuts and critical system vulnerabilities. The top leadership, both in India and overseas, knew far more than what was ever communicated to the public or even to lower-level workers at the plant. That is the stark reality of information asymmetry.

Those who had the power to act carried the burden of awareness, but not all rose to the responsibility. The tragedy wasn't just a failure of systems; it was a failure of ownership in the face of unequal knowledge. Had there been courage to confront uncomfortable truths, had responsibility matched insight, the outcome might have been different.

This is not about hoarding secrets or dramatic revelations. It's about the lived reality of decision-makers who must constantly weigh what they know against what others don't. Knowledge becomes a kind of currency, and power, but also a test of character.

The IL&FS (Infrastructure Leasing & Financial Services) crisis

The IL&FS (Infrastructure Leasing & Financial Services) crisis shook India's financial system in 2018. For years, IL&FS was viewed as a reliable name in infrastructure financing. But inside the company, signs of stress were growing. There was huge debt, low returns from projects, and lending practices that raised serious questions. A select few at the top, board members, auditors, and senior executives, had visibility into the deteriorating financial health. Yet, the external messaging remained overly optimistic, masking the risks from regulators, investors, and even government institutions.

This is information asymmetry in real time. Employees, shareholders, and the broader ecosystem believed in the stability of the company, while a handful had access to the real picture. And when the collapse happened, the impact was massive, triggering a liquidity crisis across NBFCs and shaking market confidence.

The leadership's failure was not just in financial mismanagement; it was in withholding action despite knowledge. Silence, when one holds insight that can prevent a crisis, becomes complicity.

True ownership, then, is not just doing your job well. It's carrying the invisible weight of what you know, and still choosing to act wisely. It's choosing not to weaponise knowledge, nor to hide behind it. It is neither exploitation nor abdication; it is stewardship.

This is why real leadership is lonely. The deeper your understanding, the fewer people you can share the full picture with. The paradox? You can't expect others to act with responsibility if they don't see what you see. Yet, you must still lead them forward, shaping choices, offering direction, without overwhelming them or abdicating your own deeper responsibilities.

Information asymmetry isn't going away. In fact, with the growing complexity of systems, technological, social, organisational, it's only increasing. But perhaps what we need is a culture where those who know more don't see themselves as superior, but as custodians, protectors of the whole.

Because in the end, the burden of knowing too much isn't just about facts. It's about what you choose to do with them.

5.4   *The Cursed Insight Principle*

Once You Know Something, You Can't *Unknow* It, and It Forces a Leadership Response

5.4.1

In strategy, knowledge is leverage - but not always the kind you can choose to use later. Sometimes, it arrives like a storm, uninvited, irreversible, and morally binding.

Leaders are often exposed to asymmetrical information. They notice signals that get missed, patterns others overlook, tough truths hidden in spreadsheets, or cultural undercurrents that don't match the calm surface.

The moment such knowledge crystallises, a subtle but irreversible shift takes place. What once was optional becomes imperative. This is the Cursed Insight Principle: once you know, you are no longer free not to act.

Strategic leadership, therefore, is not just about what to do, but about what to do now that you know. The cursed insight isn't a flaw in the system; it is a defining feature of authentic leadership. It is what separates those who merely occupy authority from those who bear the weight of it.

Take, for example, the early detection of a failing initiative. On paper, the project still has funding and support. Publicly, optimism is the narrative. But you've seen the early signals like misaligned KPIs, unclear ownership, a loss of momentum. At this point, your role is no longer to wait and see; it is to shift posture. To challenge. To recalibrate. To prepare the terrain for a difficult pivot. Because now you know, and with knowing comes non-delegable responsibility.

Here's the strategic dilemma: Insight without action breeds organisational decay. It signals to others, subtly but surely, that the leader is willing to look away. That hard truths can be tolerated as long as they remain inconvenient. Over time, this tolerance for cognitive dissonance infects the culture. Strategic drift sets in. Silence becomes normalised. Risk accumulates.

This principle is also relevant when leading through transformation. A leader may realise that the current business model has a two-year runway left, but saying so too early might destabilise teams. Saying it too late might doom the company. The insight is cursed not because it is wrong, but because it arrives before others are ready. That is what true strategic leadership is about. It means taking action not when it is easy or popular, but when it is truly needed.

There's no virtue in reacting to what everyone already sees. True leadership acts before the consensus. And the cursed insight is the inflection point;

it triggers the need for foresight, narrative control, and system-wide adjustment. The longer it is suppressed, the costlier the correction.

The strategic leader, therefore, must develop three capacities to navigate cursed insight:

Sense early and deeply – Build systems and personal discipline to detect weak signals and hidden patterns.

Frame insight as shared responsibility – Convert isolated knowledge into collective awareness through smart communication and engagement.

Architect timely response pathways – Don't react impulsively. Instead, design calibrated responses that de-risk transition while honouring the urgency of the truth.

The paradox is sharp: with greater perception comes constrained freedom. You cannot *unsee*. You cannot *unknow*. And you cannot delay indefinitely without consequence.

Strategic clarity, therefore, is both a gift and a burden. But this burden is not accidental; it is leadership's deepest calling.

5.4.2   Example: Kudankulam Nuclear Plant Cyberattack (2019)

In 2019, the Kudankulam Nuclear Power Plant in Tamil Nadu was reportedly targeted by a malware intrusion linked to North Korean hackers (Lazarus Group). Initially, the breach was denied. Later, it was confirmed that a non-critical administrative system was indeed compromised.

What mattered more than the breach itself was that it revealed something important. People now realised that India's critical infrastructure was vulnerable. This was no longer a theoretical cyber risk; it was real, it had happened, and it exposed systemic gaps.

This was a classic cursed insight for strategic and governmental leadership. The breach forced a recalibration of India's cyber defence posture, especially in high-value, high-risk sectors like nuclear energy, defence R&D, and financial institutions. The incident triggered silent but widespread cybersecurity reinforcements across ministries and PSUs. You couldn't *unsee* what that intrusion revealed, and ignoring it would have been strategic negligence.

The lesson: Some insights don't scream. They whisper. But even whispers, when true, demand swift architecture of resilience.

5.4.3   Reflection Questions

Have you ever held insight that others around you did not? How did you respond?

What mechanisms exist in your organisation to ensure that inconvenient knowledge leads to timely action?

How do you distinguish between uncertainty that requires caution and insight that demands urgency?

What steps can leaders take to build the moral courage needed to act on cursed insight?

In your strategic role, how do you handle the responsibility that comes with knowing more than others?

CHAPTER 6

The Illusion of Shared Ownership

When everyone owns it, no one really does.

In many modern institutions, shared ownership is promoted as a democratic ideal. It is meant to be distributed, collective, and inclusive. But beneath the surface, it often breeds ambiguity, dilutes initiative, and creates an accountability vacuum. When everyone is nominally responsible, no one feels personally answerable. This chapter dissects the fallacy of collective responsibility, where roles blur and decisions stall, revealing how group structures unintentionally enable evasion. It introduces frameworks to establish crisp accountability lines without undermining team cohesion or collaborative ethos.

6.1 The Accountability Mirage: How Collective Responsibility Dissolves Individual Action

6.1.1

There's a strangely comforting phrase that circulates in organisations, communities, and even families: *'We're all responsible'*. It sounds noble, egalitarian, even empowering. But scratch beneath the surface, and you often find something far less productive. When everyone is responsible, the accountability becomes as clear as fog, and just as slippery to hold onto. This is the accountability mirage: a convincing illusion that gives the impression of shared commitment, while in reality, it evaporates personal ownership.

We often mistake group responsibility as a higher form of maturity. But more often than not, it becomes a loophole. An emotional and structural escape hatch that allows individuals to step away from the burden of consequence. Decisions are delayed, actions diluted, and outcomes become no one's fault, but everyone's regret.

In such a system, it becomes easier to blend in than to step up. People assume someone else will take care of the problem, make the call, or clean up the mess. Ironically, even competent, driven individuals fall prey to this dynamic. Not because they are apathetic, but because the structure itself leaves room for ambiguity to take over.

This isn't merely a theoretical or philosophical concern. It's a lived reality in meetings where tasks are agreed upon but not assigned, in projects where outcomes are shared but inputs are left undefined, in cultures where failure is absorbed collectively, but learning is never owned personally.

Take a simple example: a meeting ends with a statement like *'Let's make sure the client gets the final deck by Monday.'* Everyone nods. But no one says who's actually doing it. Come Monday, the deck isn't sent. And everyone is surprised. Wasn't someone supposed to…?

That's the trap.

The group meant well. The intention was there. But intention without a clearly assigned agent becomes just a promise that quietly evaporates.

6.1.2   The Disappearing Act of Ownership

There's a psychological comfort in diffusion. Responsibility spread across a group feels less risky. There's less chance of being blamed, less chance of standing out, and paradoxically, less chance of being remembered for success. In this diffusion, people protect themselves from criticism, but they also deny themselves credit. Accountability, like oxygen, becomes scarce when it's not clearly owned.

True ownership demands clarity: *who is doing what by when.* Anything less creates a system where motion replaces action, and talk replaces traction. The moment ownership becomes collective in name only, without individual anchors, it stops being real.

The Solution: One Name, One Deadline

To break through the accountability mirage, leaders and teams must be ruthlessly specific. For every decision, assign a single owner, even when the task itself is collaborative. Make it explicit. Make it visible. Replace *'we should'* with *'you will'*. Replace *'someone needs to'* with *'Deepak will'*.

And it's not just about naming names; it's about creating a culture that respects and supports that clarity. Ownership should be seen not as a burden but as a badge. When individuals know what they are responsible for, and that they are trusted to see it through, they are more likely to step forward, not shrink away.

6.1.3   A Deeper Leadership Responsibility

Leaders play a pivotal role here. In the name of teamwork, many leaders avoid assigning individual ownership because they fear seeming autocratic or overly directive. Ironically, their reluctance to assign accountability is the very thing that weakens the team. Empowering individuals doesn't mean removing clarity; it means reinforcing it.

Creating a culture of real ownership means removing the illusion that accountability can float in a vacuum. It can't. It always needs a home. Someone who gives it a name, a voice, and says, *'Yes, I've got this.'*

6.1.4   Case Example: The 2020 Migrant Labour Crisis During COVID-19 Lockdown

When the nationwide lockdown was announced in March 2020 with just a few hours' notice, India's vast population of internal migrant workers were suddenly stranded. These are the people who build our cities and keep essential services running. With transportation suspended and no clear communication or coordination, millions were left to walk hundreds of kilometers home, often with no food, shelter, or money. Some died on the way. Many suffered in silence.

In the public narrative that followed, there was widespread condemnation, but also an eerie absence of specific accountability. The Centre said states were responsible for implementation. States said the Centre hadn't given adequate notice or support. Railways said they were waiting for state approvals. Local authorities claimed they weren't informed. At its core, everyone was supposed to own it, but no one truly did.

The crisis unfolded not because of bad intent but because of fractured ownership. When responsibility is too broadly shared across layers of government and institutions without clearly defined roles and outcomes, it creates the illusion that *someone must be handling it*. Meanwhile, real human consequences unfold in the background.

6.2   Committees, Boards, and Blame: The Architecture of Indecision

6.2.1

At first glance, committees and boards appear to be the very embodiment of collective wisdom. They bring together diverse perspectives, specialised knowledge, and institutional experience. In theory, they are supposed to sharpen decisions through debate, challenge groupthink, and democratise power. But in practice, they often end up doing the exact opposite.

The moment responsibility turns into a group activity, ownership starts to blur. Without a clear, single owner, decision-making becomes a roundabout. There's movement, but no real direction. Accountability floats in the air, unable to land.

Ask anyone who has been on a corporate committee or board during a crisis, and they'll tell you it's often the place where clarity fades and blame gets passed around. Decisions are delayed, deflected, or diluted. No one wants to take the first step, lest they also be left holding the bag if things go wrong.

The architecture of these bodies, committees, boards, panels, is rarely built for speed or ownership. They are designed to protect, not propel. Every resolution is layered with caveats. Every bold idea is tamed by compromise. And every failure is conveniently attributed to 'the collective'.

In organisational psychology, this phenomenon is called diffusion of responsibility. The more people involved in a decision, the less personally responsible each one feels. It's a cognitive loophole through which inaction slips, unnoticed.

Worse, these structures often create a theatre of action. Agendas are drawn, minutes recorded, discussions held. And yet, the real decisions are either avoided or made elsewhere. Behind closed doors, or not made at all. What remains is the illusion of process, not the substance of progress.

To be clear, the problem isn't with collaboration or consultation. Both are vital. The problem is with abdicated responsibility disguised as shared leadership. A committee can advise, even challenge, but someone must ultimately own the call. A board can oversee, but someone must steer.

True leadership doesn't hide behind plurality. It emerges from clarity. It says, *"I will take the call"*, not *"Let's see what the group thinks"*. It understands that while shared input enriches decisions, shared ownership, when unchecked, can erode them.

In the end, *the paradox is simple yet damning*: when everyone is technically responsible, no one feels personally accountable. And when no one feels accountable, decisions either don't happen or happen without conviction.

That's not leadership. That's architecture built for indecision, and, worse, for blame.

6.2.2   Case Example: The Nirbhaya Fund – A Promise Lost in Process

In 2013, after the horrific Delhi gang rape incident that shook the conscience of the nation, the Government of India created the Nirbhaya Fund, a ₹1,000 crore corpus intended to enhance the safety and dignity of women. It was a powerful gesture that carried the promise of decisive action.

But over the years, the fund has become a classic example of how good intentions collapse under the weight of indecision and scattered accountability.

Multiple ministries, Home, Women and Child Development, Road Transport, Railways, were made stakeholders. States were asked to submit proposals. Approvals had to pass through several layers of committees. As a result, the disbursement remained painfully slow, and large portions of the fund remained unutilised even years after its creation.

Everyone was 'involved' in managing the fund, but no one owned its outcomes. Ministries blamed states. States blamed unclear guidelines. Proposals languished in files. And the very purpose of the fund, swift, meaningful action to protect women, got buried under administrative machinery.

A fund created in response to public outrage became a symbol of institutional lethargy, not because of lack of resources, but because of lack of ownership.

Ref: https://www.cbgaindia.org/blog/nirbhaya-fund-could-help-improve-womens-safety-but-money-allotted-for-schemes-is-underutilised/

https://www.business-standard.com/article/economy-policy/nearly-half-of-nirbhaya-funds-unutilised-shows-data-122032100809_1

When responsibility is sliced into too many hands, even urgent justice gets lost in paperwork.

6.3 Designing Clarity in Group Ownership Without Diluting Leadership

6.3.1

When we say 'we're all responsible', it often sounds noble. As if we've reached some utopian ideal of collective commitment. Yet, more often than not, this well-meaning phrase dissolves accountability instead of strengthening it. The intention is unity, but the outcome is usually ambiguity.

In group ownership, the critical challenge lies in preserving clarity without neutering leadership. Without a clear framework, shared ownership turns into a fog where everyone assumes someone else is steering the ship.

Group ownership is not the same as leadership by committee. The latter often leads to indecision, diluted authority, and ultimately, inertia. But when designed thoughtfully, group ownership can coexist with strong leadership. The key is to design systems where everyone knows what they own, why it matters, and who leads the charge when alignment wavers.

6.3.2   Ownership with Edges

Imagine a puzzle. Each piece is distinct but interlocks with others to complete the picture. That's how shared ownership needs to be structured. Ownership with clear edges.. Everyone contributes, but each person or team owns a well-defined segment. This doesn't restrict collaboration; it enables it. Because people are clearer about where their responsibility begins and ends, they can more confidently engage others without stepping on toes or shrugging off decisions.

This kind of design demands upfront clarity:

Who owns the final call?

Who is accountable for outcomes?

Where is collaboration welcomed but not compulsory?

What happens when there's disagreement or drift?

These questions are not bureaucratic; they're liberating. They prevent the chaos of collective ambiguity.

6.3.3   Leadership as the Anchor

Strong leadership in shared ownership models isn't about controlling every decision. It's about anchoring purpose and creating alignment. A good leader ensures that no one's role becomes invisible in the crowd and that the edges of ownership are respected and reinforced.

When group ownership is working, the leader doesn't micromanage. Instead, they curate clarity, fuel momentum, and intervene only when the structure is wobbling or drifting. They don't take over. They reinforce direction.

The paradox is this: the more clarity you bring to group ownership, the less you need to control, and the more leadership is felt, not forced.

6.3.4   Guardrails, Not Gridlocks

To avoid diluting leadership, it's critical to set up guardrails rather than gridlocks. Guardrails offer boundaries and clarity but allow for speed and fluidity. Everyone knows the rules of engagement, the shared goal, and the latitude within which they can innovate.

In the absence of guardrails, teams often default to two extremes: either paralysing over-collaboration (where every decision is a group project) or defensive *siloing* (where people hoard control to protect themselves from blame). Both erode shared ownership and cloud leadership.

6.3.5   Building a Culture of Mutual Stewardship

Ultimately, sustainable group ownership emerges from culture - not just structure. It's about creating a shared sense of stewardship where everyone feels psychologically safe to own, act, and speak up, knowing that leadership is both present and empowering.

When you design for clarity in ownership and strength in leadership, you don't dilute either; you amplify both.

The message then shifts from *'we all own this'* (a statement of vague hope) to:

'I own my part, you own yours, and together we advance, anchored by leadership, guided by clarity'.

That is when group ownership transcends illusion and becomes a powerful engine of collective accountability.

6.3.6   Structuring Accountability Without Bureaucracy

Here's a sharp, real-world insight, and one that many institutions grapple with silently.

Committees are often formed for specific purposes, drawing personnel from multiple departments to benefit from cross-functional expertise. However, a common structural problem gets in the way. The members usually don't report to each other, and the most senior person is named the committee head but doesn't have real authority over the others.

The committee head usually does not influence the annual performance evaluations of the members, which leads to a lack of direct accountability. As a result, members may not feel a strong sense of responsibility toward the committee or its head.

This absence of hierarchical clarity and performance linkage often leads to delays in proceedings, dilution of focus, inconclusive discussions, and poor implementation of decisions. When ownership is unclear and accountability is diffused, the committee risks becoming a symbolic forum rather than a vehicle for decisive action.

Similarly, matrix organisational structures, where team members report to multiple leaders, frequently struggle to deliver consistent results due to unclear authority and competing priorities. A more effective alternative lies in project-based teams comprising cross-functional members who report directly to a designated Project Head with formal authority. This clear chain of command bestows stronger ownership, better coordination, and more effective execution.

Solution: Embedding Authority and Accountability into Collaborative Structures

To ensure that committees and cross-functional teams function effectively, it is essential to move beyond symbolic collaboration and establish structures that promote both clarity and accountability.

1. Define Clear Mandates and Deliverables

Each committee or team should operate under a formally defined Terms of Reference (ToR), clearly outlining:

The objective and scope of work

Specific deliverables and timelines

Individual responsibilities and expected contributions

Decision-making authority and escalation protocols

This transforms the group from a loose assembly into a results-oriented unit with measurable outcomes.

2. Delegate Formal Authority to the Chair or Project Head

The effectiveness of any cross-functional team depends on the presence of formal authority. The Committee Head or Project Head must be granted clear and recognised decision-making powers within the scope of the assignment. This includes:

Authority to assign tasks and monitor progress

The ability to escalate delays or non-compliance

Endorsement from senior leadership to reinforce legitimacy

Such authority prevents the dilution of leadership and ensures alignment across functional boundaries.

3. Establish Temporary Reporting Structures

Where traditional reporting lines do not exist, introduce a temporary functional reporting framework for the duration of the committee or project. Team members remain attached to their departments but are accountable to the designated head for all matters related to the assigned task. This reinforces responsibility without disrupting the parent department's structure.

4. Link Participation to Performance Evaluations

To drive engagement, contributions to cross-functional initiatives should be reflected in individual performance appraisals. This could be done through:

Defined KPIs related to committee or project outcomes

Inputs from the Committee or Project Head to the member's appraisal

Recognition, awards, or visibility for effective participation

When individuals know their performance matters beyond their routine roles, motivation increases significantly.

5. Appoint a Dedicated Coordinator or Secretariat

A supporting coordinator or secretariat ensures administrative efficiency by:

Scheduling meetings and tracking attendance

Maintaining records and minutes

Following up on assigned actions and progress

This role anchors the team's momentum and prevents operational drift.

6. Ensure Structured Closure and Implementation Follow-Up

Committees and project teams should not disband with the submission of a report or recommendation. Instead, there must be:

A formal review or presentation to leadership

An actionable implementation plan with clearly assigned responsibilities

Periodic review checkpoints to track execution and outcomes

This ensures continuity and accountability beyond the discussion stage.

7. Prefer Project-Based Teams Over Matrix Structures

While matrix organisations aim for flexibility, they often lead to confusion in authority and prioritisation. Wherever possible, assign dedicated project-based teams where all members report directly to a Project Head with formal control over task execution. This promotes unified direction, sharper focus, and faster decision-making.

In summary: Collaborative structures succeed not by intention alone but by design. Authority must be explicit, roles must be clear, and accountability must be embedded. When these elements are aligned, committees and cross-functional teams evolve from passive forums into powerful engines of execution.

6.3.7 Case Example: From a Stalled Steering Committee to a High-Performance Project Team

At a prominent public sector shipbuilding company, a Steering Committee was formed to oversee the adoption of a new enterprise resource planning (ERP) system. The committee comprised senior representatives from departments like Finance, Materials, Production, and IT. Though cross-functional expertise was present, the members did not formally report to the Committee Chair, and none were evaluated based on the committee's performance. Meetings were irregular, decisions were deferred, and progress stagnated. Despite multiple rounds of discussions, the ERP implementation remained on paper.

Recognising the inertia, senior management restructured the initiative into a time-bound project. A full-time Project Head was appointed, with delegated authority to direct team members drawn from various departments. Team members were temporarily assigned to the project, with performance metrics linked to implementation milestones. A dedicated project office with support staff was set up to drive coordination, document decisions, and track progress.

The transformation was immediate. With clear accountability, empowered leadership, and visible timelines, the project gained momentum. Within months, critical modules were piloted, training schedules rolled out, and integration plans executed. The ERP system went live within the revised timeframe.

Lesson: The same people, when moved from a symbolic committee to a formally empowered project structure, delivered transformative results. The difference lay not in intent, but in the clarity of leadership, structure, and ownership.

CHAPTER 7

Ownership by Proxy: The Ethics of Delegated Authority

You can delegate the task, but not the consequence.

Leaders often act through others, like assistants, deputies, consultants. But delegation doesn't lift the moral or strategic weight from the one who made the decision. In reality, responsibility lingers with the one who empowered, not merely the one who executed. This chapter explores the layered ethics of proxy decision-making, unpacking how invisible lines of influence and trust can both empower and entrap. It presents case patterns where decisions made by others in your name ricochet back with unintended consequences, offering strategies for oversight without micromanagement.

7.1 The Silent Command: How Delegation Reshapes Ethical Responsibility

7.1.1

People often talk about delegation as a way to manage workload. It helps share tasks, spread the effort, and get more done. But underneath, something deeper is happening. There's a quiet shift in who holds the ethical responsibility. It is a silent command; issued not just to complete a task, but to bear the moral weight of choices made in someone else's name.

When a leader delegates, they do not simply ask for something to be done. They entrust judgment, discretion, and decision-making. They give another person the power to act as them, or for them. In doing so, they are not abdicating responsibility; they are multiplying it, dispersing it across invisible threads of trust, competence, and alignment. These threads are not always visible, but they are always binding.

Delegation, then, is not the shedding of responsibility; it is its diffusion. What changes is not whether responsibility exists, but where it lives, and how it evolves in transit.

7.1.2   The Ethical Mirage

A risky belief often comes with delegation. People start thinking that once a task is handed over, all the ethical responsibility belongs to the person doing it. That illusion is seductive. It allows us to say, *'They handled it'*, or *'It wasn't my call'*, when outcomes turn sour. But if leadership means anything, it means remaining answerable for what happens in our name, even when we are not directly involved.

When a ship veers off course, the captain cannot point to the helmsman alone. Authority was delegated; ownership was not.

7.1.3   The Double-Edged Trust

Delegation, at its best, is a gesture of empowerment. It says, I trust you. But trust is never neutral - it imposes its own moral structure. When someone is trusted with power, they often carry not just the burden of executing, but of interpreting the values behind the mission. They must infer what the leader would want: *what is acceptable, what is off-limits, what trade-offs are tolerable.*

This inference is where ethics begins to bend. Delegation creates distance, and distance blurs clarity. A well-meaning subordinate may act with technical excellence but moral misalignment. Not because they are unethical, but because they never heard the silent values behind the silent command.

The leader remains responsible, not just for the outcomes, but for the silence.

7.1.4   Ethical Echoes and Unspoken Signals

Every delegation carries hidden signals. When a manager says, 'Just get it done', but rewards speed over scrutiny, they are silently sanctioning shortcuts. When they say, 'Use your judgment', without articulating what principles should guide that judgment, they invite ambiguity.

Ethical leadership requires more than clear tasks; it demands clear tone. Delegation without moral framing is like giving a compass without a true north. The task may be completed, but the direction may be wrong.

7.1.5   Responsibility That Cannot Be Outsourced

At its core, ownership by proxy is an inescapable paradox. You can delegate authority, but you cannot delegate conscience. You can assign roles, but not erase your role in shaping the environment where choices are made.

This is especially critical in organisations, where power is often layered, and decisions ripple far from the original intent. A leader may never sign the contract, authorise the payment, or write the report, but their fingerprints are on the culture that did.

This is why leaders must stay ethically present even when operationally distant. The higher the position, the more silent the commands, and the louder their consequences.

7.1.6   Case Study: The NEET Exam Paper Leak – When Delegation Becomes Ethical Abdication

In 2023, the National Eligibility cum Entrance Test (NEET) for undergraduate medical courses, one of India's most high-stakes entrance exams, was marred by a paper leak scandal. The breach didn't just expose a flaw in the examination system; it revealed the brittle chain of delegated responsibility, where ethics were assumed but not ensured.

The National Testing Agency (NTA), entrusted with conducting the exam, had outsourced key aspects of logistics and security to third-party vendors. These vendors, in turn, delegated further. They brought in local staff, transporters, and temporary workers to handle the papers securely. Somewhere in this vast maze of delegation, vigilance blurred, and a silent compromise took root.

The paper leak was not a failure of individual vigilance alone; it was a systemic failure of ethical oversight across layers of delegated authority. Every link in the chain believed someone else was ultimately responsible. But for the students, lakhs of them, the consequences were devastating. Their hopes were crushed, results put on hold, and trust completely shaken.

What this incident starkly illustrates is that ethical responsibility does not dilute with each layer of delegation; it accumulates. When leadership at the top fails to ensure moral clarity, institutional culture, and robust accountability in the delegation process, they don't just risk operational breakdown; they risk public trust.

The silent command here was not just the logistical directive to conduct an exam; it was the ethical silence on how it must be conducted.

7.2 Surrogate Decision-Making: When Others Act in Your Name

7.2.1

There is a strange vulnerability in watching someone make a decision that will bear your name but not your fingerprints. The moment we delegate authority, whether to a subordinate, a proxy, or even an automated system, we step into a moral and strategic paradox. We entrust, and yet we remain entangled.

Surrogate decision-making is not simply about handing over the reins; it's about navigating the delicate tension between trust and accountability. In leadership, it's rarely feasible to make every call personally. So we designate others to act on our behalf. But when decisions are made in our name, the consequences, good or bad, still come home to us. The credit might be shared. The blame? Not always.

This paradox reveals itself most acutely in crisis situations. A diplomat negotiates under the authority of a head of state. A doctor makes life-altering decisions for a patient who cannot respond. A ship captain authorises a junior officer to take charge in high seas. These moments are shaped not only by competence but by conscience. The surrogate must act not as themselves, but as a moral and strategic extension of the principal.

Yet here's the challenge. No matter how much we train, guide, or trust the surrogate, they remain, by definition, another person, with their own instincts, experiences, and ethical compass.

Their decision may reflect your intent, or diverge from it. The closer the alignment between your values and theirs, the more seamless the handover. But the greater the gap, the higher the cost of misjudgment.

This raises a deeper question. To what extent are we responsible for the decisions made by those who represent us?

Legally, perhaps there are boundaries. But ethically, the ownership rarely diffuses. If a team member fails to uphold your standards while acting on your behalf, it isn't enough to say, *"That wasn't me."* Because it was, through your appointment, your delegation, your lack of oversight, or your silence.

On the other hand, to micromanage is to breed mediocrity. Leadership demands the humility to trust others and the foresight to prepare them. *The paradox is this:* empowering others is necessary for growth and scale, but it never absolves you of what they do in your name.

This section of ownership by proxy forces us to reflect not only on whom we choose to speak or act for us, but also how we equip them. It's not just about delegation. It's about transference of judgment, values, and responsibility. Every surrogate decision becomes a test of how well you've prepared the ecosystem around you to think, decide, and lead in your absence.

The wise leader, then, does not merely appoint representatives; they develop custodians. People who understand the gravity of the role, the weight of the name they carry, and the quiet accountability that follows.

Because in the end, when others act in your name, the decision may be theirs, but the ownership, unmistakably, is still yours.

7.2.2   Illustration: The 2G Spectrum Allocation Scandal – When Authority Was Delegated but Accountability Was Elusive

One of the most telling examples of surrogate decision-making, and its ethical consequences, was the 2G spectrum allocation scandal that rocked India in the late 2000s. At the heart of the controversy was the delegation of authority by the Union Government to the Department of Telecommunications (DoT), specifically under then-Minister A. Raja. The allocation of spectrum licenses, allegedly at throwaway prices, raised questions about policy manipulation, cronyism, and massive revenue loss.

The deeper concern, however, lay in the nature of how decisions were made and who ultimately owned them. Ministerial powers were exercised, but within the framework set by higher authorities - rules framed, timelines approved, and oversight (or the lack thereof) tolerated. When the scandal broke, political leadership at the highest levels claimed no direct involvement, stating that procedures were delegated and decisions taken by departments.

But can power be delegated without consequence? And more importantly, can responsibility be outsourced when decisions are made in your name?

The aftermath of the scandal saw not only a legal and institutional fallout, but also an erosion of public trust. While some individuals were acquitted in court due to lack of evidence or procedural lapses, the reputational damage to institutions and individuals was long-lasting. The broader message was unmistakable. Delegation without due diligence is not empowerment; it is abdication.

This case serves as a grim reminder that when systems are loosely monitored, and proxies act without ethical alignment, the eventual accountability boomerangs on those at the top. Surrogate decision-making, especially in public institutions, demands not just clear instructions, but unwavering vigilance.

7.3 *Building Proxy-Responsibility Models Without Moral Disengagement*

7.3.1

Delegation is not abdication. And yet, in the modern architecture of organisations, be it in corporate structures, governments, or even families, the convenient illusion that 'someone else is responsible now' has allowed moral disengagement to quietly fester.

We must ask: When authority is delegated, can responsibility truly be outsourced? Or is it merely redistributed, with its moral weight still subtly tethered to the original source?

To build proxy-responsibility models that do not invite moral apathy, we must rethink the design of delegation. Authority given to others must carry not just the power to decide, but the ethics to decide well.

1. Clarify What Cannot Be Delegated

At the heart of any responsible model lies clarity. Certain responsibilities, especially those that pertain to values, fairness, and long-term consequences, should remain non-transferable. A CEO can delegate decisions, but cannot outsource the integrity of the company. A military commander may issue operational command, but not moral intent.

By identifying what is inherently yours to bear, leaders avoid the dangerous assumption that power transferred equals burden erased.

2. Embed Reflection in the Chain of Command

Too often, proxy models are built on efficiency and compliance. But thinking ethically may seem slow, yet it's what truly guides good decisions. Leaders must embed reflective checkpoints, moments where both the delegator and the proxy decision-maker pause to ask, *"Is this the right thing to do, not just the logical or profitable one?"*

This could be through scenario-based reviews, ethical audits, or simply a culture that encourages second thoughts and conscientious dissent. When a junior team member hesitates to follow a directive that 'doesn't feel right', they are not slowing the system; they are strengthening its spine.

3. Create Shared Ownership, Not Shifting Blame

The structure of shared ownership is different from diluted ownership. In a diluted model, everyone claims they're only doing their part, and no one feels fully accountable for the result. But in a shared model, everyone holds a piece of the outcome's moral fabric.

A strong proxy-responsibility system ensures that while the person executing the task has autonomy, the person delegating it remains emotionally and ethically involved. It's not just about who does it, but who cares about what is done.

4. Make Ethics Visible in Metrics

What gets measured gets managed. But what gets felt gets upheld. Proxy systems often fail because their success is measured only in KPIs, like timelines met, costs saved, targets achieved. But where is the space to measure harm avoided, dignity preserved, trust earned?

To prevent moral disengagement, responsibility must be built into the metrics, tracking not just what was done, but how it was done and at what ethical cost.

5. Reinforce the Emotional Link to Outcomes

Detachment is the breeding ground of disengagement. When proxy decision-makers feel no emotional consequence of their actions, when the outcome seems distant, abstract, or someone else's problem, ethics are the first casualty.

Leaders must consciously reconnect people with purpose. Every proxy action must be tied to its real-world impact, on people, on communities, on the brand's soul. Storytelling, feedback loops, even symbolic rituals can help reinforce that every act done in proxy is still an act done in our name.

7.3.2   The Invisible Thread

True delegation, then, is not the act of handing over responsibility, but of lending trust while retaining moral commitment. Proxy-responsibility models work not because the system is clever, but because the people in it are consciously awake to their inescapable roles.

We build systems. Systems shape behaviour. But unless systems are designed with moral continuity in mind, we risk creating intelligent machines operated by ethically disconnected humans.

Leadership today is not about how well we hand over control; it is about how deeply we remain connected to the consequences.

7.3.3 Chilling Example: The Post-Midday Meal Tragedy in Bihar (2013)

When Operational Delegation Meets Moral Blindness

In July 2013, a tragic incident shook the conscience of the nation when 23 children died after consuming a contaminated midday meal at a government primary school in Gandaman village, Bihar. The food was laced with monocrotophos, a highly toxic pesticide, believed to have been in the cooking oil.

On paper, the system had all the necessary elements:

A government scheme to provide nutrition to underprivileged children.

Local procurement and decentralised execution to ensure flexibility and local employment.

School authorities designated as nodal delivery points.

But the tragedy occurred because the chain of delegated responsibility lacked moral supervision at every link.

The school principal, who also procured the oil, reportedly ignored warnings from the cook about its foul smell. The local administration had no mechanism to monitor the quality of food being served daily. The education department treated the scheme as a compliance checklist, while the broader system saw it as a delivery function, not a duty of care.

What failed was not just hygiene; it was empathy.

No one in the chain of command asked the human question: *"Would I serve this food to my own children?"*

This is where moral disengagement in proxy models becomes deadly. Everyone has a title, a task, a target, but no one has a sense of moral intimacy with the outcome.

The Lesson: This tragedy illustrates how proxy-responsibility models can collapse catastrophically when execution is divorced from ethical engagement. Authority can be passed down; but ownership of impact must remain shared and sacred.

CHAPTER 8

Emotional Ownership: The Unseen Weight Leaders Carry

What you feel responsible for matters as much as what you actually are.

There's a kind of responsibility that doesn't show up on balance sheets or org charts. It's the emotional load of leadership. Leaders often internalise more than their official scope, carrying unspoken worries, personal regrets, and a silent sense of duty to people and causes beyond their remit. This chapter shines a light on emotional ownership - the type driven by care, conscience, and internal narrative rather than formal designation. It explores how over-identification with outcomes can lead to burnout and decision distortion, and how to calibrate empathy without losing effectiveness.

8.1 *The Guilt Gap: When Leaders Carry Emotional Burdens They Can't Justify Logically*

Leadership, at its core, is not just about decisions, outcomes, or responsibilities. It's about people. It's about promises, some made out loud, others whispered silently in a leader's own mind. Somewhere between what we do and what we hope to do, between how things are and how we wish they were, there's a strange weight we carry. It's guilt without logic. Emotional ownership of things leaders were never meant to own.

This is the guilt gap.

It is the quiet ache that doesn't show up on performance reviews or balance sheets. The kind of guilt that emerges not from wrongdoing, but from a haunting feeling that somehow, somewhere, a leader should have done more, known better, acted sooner, or prevented the hurt. Even if the facts, the timelines, and the reality clearly say, *"It wasn't your fault"*.

This guilt is not always rational - it rarely is. But it's real. And it takes up residence in the emotional vaults of conscientious leaders.

8.1.1   The Weight of Being the Anchor

To lead is to become the anchor of a ship. Steady and grounding, yet exposed to tides that no one else feels. When things go wrong in a team, or someone underperforms, or a talented person burns out and leaves, many leaders instinctively ask: *What could I have done differently?*

Even when they did everything they could.

Sometimes, it's the burden of seeing someone's potential fall through the cracks. Or watching a project fail despite the team's best efforts. Or realising that while you were putting out strategic fires, someone in the team was struggling silently. The logical mind might say, *"You can't be everywhere,"* but the heart counters, *"Still, I wish I had been."*

It is not just responsibility; it is emotional entanglement.

8.1.2   Why It Hurts More Than It Should

There's a subtle, almost invisible moral contract that deeply empathetic leaders sign, often unknowingly. It says: *"If people around me suffer, I must carry some of that weight."* This doesn't come from arrogance. It comes from care. From empathy. From a desire to lead not just efficiently, but ethically, humanly.

But here's the paradox: the more you care, the more likely you are to carry guilt that doesn't belong to you. And ironically, that very guilt can cloud your leadership. It can make you hesitate, second-guess, or stretch yourself too thin trying to prevent future pain, becoming reactive rather than proactive.

It's a noble instinct. But unchecked, it is self-defeating.

8.1.3   Emotional Debts That No One Asked You to Pay

Often, leaders pay emotional debts that no one else even remembers. A passing remark from a disengaged team member becomes a source of internal inquiry. A delayed recognition for someone's effort haunts the leader far longer than it matters to the person involved. Sometimes, a team member's personal hardship can weigh on a leader's heart as if it were a managerial failure rather than a human challenge.

This is what makes the guilt gap so elusive. It is not triggered by failure alone, but by the perception of falling short, in any emotional or moral sense.

8.1.4   Closing the Gap Without Closing Your Heart

So how do leaders deal with this? How do you continue to feel deeply and lead authentically, without being consumed by emotional burdens you cannot resolve?

It begins with recognising that emotional ownership must have boundaries. Compassion is essential. So is responsibility. But so is the wisdom to know where your circle of control ends and where another's agency begins.

You are not responsible for every outcome, only for the integrity of your intention and the sincerity of your effort.

Leaders need time to reflect, not to hide their guilt, but to understand it. They should ask themselves, *"Is this guilt pushing me to grow, or is it just sadness disguised as responsibility?"* That difference matters. Because not every emotional weight needs to be shouldered. Some simply need to be acknowledged, honoured, and gently put down.

8.1.5   The Unseen Mark of Mature Leadership

Perhaps the truest mark of mature leadership is not perfection, nor omnipresence, but the ability to lead with full-hearted presence, while accepting that some things will always remain out of reach.

To be accountable, yet not self-punishing.

To be emotionally aware, yet not emotionally entangled.

To walk with empathy, yet not drown in others' struggles.

That is the delicate art of leading through the guilt gap.

8.1.6   Reflection: The Silent Rooms of Leadership

Every leader walks through silent rooms no one else sees.

Rooms filled not with applause or accolades, but with second-guessing, unspoken regrets, and the emotional echoes of decisions made in good faith. In these quiet corners of leadership, guilt sometimes lingers, not because you failed, but because you cared.

But guilt is not always a signal of wrongdoing. Sometimes, it is simply the scar tissue of responsibility worn too close to the heart.

In learning to lead, we must also learn to let go. Not of accountability, but of the illusion that we can fix, foresee, or feel everything on behalf of everyone.

Let your care remain strong. Let your conscience stay awake.

But remember that even the strongest shoulders need rest, and not every burden was yours to begin with.

8.2   Case Studies

Case 1: The SLV-3 Failure – Carrying the Burden Alone

In 1979, India's first Satellite Launch Vehicle (SLV-3), which Dr. Kalam led as project director, failed just moments after take-off. The rocket veered off course and had to be destroyed mid-air. It was a devastating moment for the Indian space programme.

Despite the fact that it was a team effort and there were multiple technical reasons for the failure, Dr. Kalam personally internalised the failure, standing in front of the nation and accepting full responsibility.

But here's the deeper emotional layer:

Prof. Satish Dhawan, the ISRO Chairman, had instructed Dr. Kalam to face the media and own the failure, which he did, taking all the blame on his shoulders.

A year later, in 1980, when the same SLV project succeeded and India launched its first satellite into orbit, Dhawan called the media himself and made Dr. Kalam stand beside him, and gave him full credit in front of the world.

Dr. Kalam later reflected on this moment as a lesson in leadership, but he also expressed how he spent nights questioning what he missed, how he could've foreseen it, and how he let his team and country down, even though the failure wasn't solely his to bear.

The Guilt Gap

The Guilt Was Not Logical: Technically, he had done everything within his control. It was a system failure, not personal negligence.

The Burden Was Emotional: Yet, he carried the weight alone, driven by a deep sense of commitment to his team, his country, and his own moral compass.

He Anchored Others' Hopes: His sense of guilt came not from wrongdoing, but from disappointing the hopes placed in him.

He Grew Through It: Dr. Kalam used this as a moment of growth, but the scar of that emotional ownership stayed with him.

Insight for Leaders

Just like described in The Guilt Gap, Dr. Kalam's leadership showcases how leaders often carry unassigned emotional debts, not because they are responsible in the legal or formal sense, but because their heart signs a silent contract of care.

And often, that contract is honoured in silence, in the 'rooms no one else sees'.

Case 2: Shri Ratan Tata and the Tata Nano – A Dream that Turned into a Silent Burden

In the mid-2000s, Shri Ratan Tata launched the Tata Nano, famously dubbed the 'People's Car'. It was a bold vision. The aim was to give Indian families a safe and affordable car when most could only afford a two-wheeler.

Tata poured his personal credibility into the project. The Nano plant in Singur, West Bengal became a battleground of politics, protests, and public emotion. When land acquisition issues forced Tata Motors to pull out, the company had to relocate the entire project to Sanand, Gujarat, at great cost and disruption.

Despite heroic engineering and a rapid shift, Nano failed to meet sales expectations. It was misperceived as a 'cheap' car rather than an 'affordable' one, hurting both aspirations and market acceptance.

But here's what makes it a classic example of 'The Guilt Gap':

Rationally Right, Emotionally Heavy

Intent was noble: Provide dignity and safety to millions of Indians.

Strategy was sound: Low-cost innovation, frugal engineering, national pride.

Execution was swift: Rebuilt entire facilities in record time.

Yet, when the project didn't succeed, Shri Ratan Tata shouldered the emotional weight, not just as a business leader, but as someone who felt he had let down a dream - a dream shared by engineers, workers, dealers, and aspiring Indian families.

He wasn't blamed. Shareholders and media moved on. But Shri Ratan Tata still carried the emotional residue of the Nano.

The Guilt Gap

Nobody blamed Ratan Tata; he didn't do anything wrong. Yet, he blamed himself.

He made every correct decision under the circumstances, but the emotional promise of the project still weighed on him.

It's a textbook case of how a leader can be guiltless in action, but not in emotion.

Insight for the Leader

The Nano story teaches that true leaders don't just calculate outcomes; they absorb emotion.

They often feel guilt not for failing, but for not delivering on shared hopes.

And this silent guilt is rarely spoken of, but it defines the emotional cost of leadership.

8.3   Compassion Fatigue in Ownership: Caring Too Much, Too Often

No one warns leaders about the cost of caring.

It begins innocently, even nobly. You start with empathy, with listening, with being present, not just for the tasks, but for the people. You understand that leadership isn't just about performance metrics; it's about human moments. And so, you give. Your time, your attention, your emotional bandwidth.

But what happens when the giving doesn't stop? When caring becomes constant? When you take on not just the problems you're meant to solve, but also the pain you're never meant to carry alone?

That's when the soul starts to tire.

It doesn't happen with a dramatic breakdown. It's quieter than that. Subtler. One day, you realise your responses are shorter, your patience thinner, your energy lower. You feel a strange numbness where there was once warmth. You find yourself avoiding that one more conversation, that one more check-in, because deep down, you know your emotional tank is empty.

This is compassion fatigue. And for leaders who live in the realm of emotional ownership, it is all too common, and rarely spoken about.

8.3.1   When Empathy Becomes Exhaustion

Caring is part of leadership. But what happens when you care too often, for too long, without replenishing yourself? Compassion, once your greatest strength, begins to feel like a weight. A duty. A quiet pressure to always be the emotional sponge in the room.

And paradoxically, the very things that made you a good leader can slowly begin to erode your capacity to lead well. Your ability to understand, to stay present, and to care deeply starts to take a toll over time.

Empathy without recovery leads to emotional erosion. You become a shadow of your fuller self, present, but no longer engaged. Available, but no longer alive to the moment.

This feeling of exhaustion isn't just physical tiredness. It's the soul gently asking for rest.

8.3.2   The Hidden Cost of Being 'The One Everyone Turns To'

Many leaders, especially those with deep emotional intelligence, become the unofficial counsellors, the sounding boards, the safe space for their teams. People come not just with problems, but with pain. And because you care, you listen. You absorb. You reassure. Again and again.

But slowly, unknowingly, you begin to hold space for everyone but yourself.

You begin to carry others' grief without having the time to process your own.

You begin to normalise your own burnout because it feels selfish to step away when others are struggling.

This cycle is not sustainable. And what makes it worse is that most leaders caught in it rarely ask for help, because they've built their identity around being the one who gives it.

8.3.3   Healthy Boundaries Are Not a Lack of Compassion

Caring deeply does not mean caring endlessly.

It's possible to lead with heart and still have emotional boundaries. To show up for your people and still carve out time to return to yourself.

To hold space for others without becoming a storage container for unresolved emotions.

Setting boundaries doesn't mean you care less. It means you care wisely.

Because the more depleted you are, the less effective your compassion becomes. What starts as empathy slowly turns into irritability or a sense of distance. Sometimes it becomes emotional disconnection that looks like calm strength on the outside.

8.3.4   Refilling the Inner Well

Leaders must learn to refill their inner well before it runs dry.

This doesn't always mean grand sabbaticals or retreats. Sometimes, it's as simple as:

Taking five minutes of solitude between meetings to breathe and reset.

Saying 'not now' without guilt when your emotional reserves are low.

Having your safe space, a mentor, friend, coach, or journal, to release what you've absorbed.

Allowing yourself to feel tired without shaming yourself for it.

Caring is a gift. But even gifts, when overextended, become burdens.

Let your compassion be a renewable energy, not a one-time fuel. And remember that the people you lead need your presence, not your emotional martyrdom.

8.3.5   Reflection: The Fire That Needs Tending

Compassion is a fire. It warms, it lights, it transforms.

But even fire, when left untended, flickers and fades. Or worse; it burns out the very vessel that holds it.

As leaders, we often forget that we, too, are human. That we cannot pour endlessly from an empty cup. That care, to remain meaningful, must be replenished with rest, boundaries, and self-compassion.

You are not failing your people by protecting your energy. You are preserving your ability to show up for them tomorrow.

Tend to your inner fire, not just so you can keep leading, but so you can keep loving the very act of leadership itself.

Recommended Reading: My Charioteer Ch 12: Compassion – paragraph on Self-Compassion

8.4   Balancing Empathy with Operational Detachment

Leadership often feels like walking a tightrope between heart and head.

On one side is empathy, the ability to truly see, hear, and feel with your people. It's what builds trust, fuels belonging, and creates cultures where people don't just survive, but thrive.

On the other side is operational detachment, the cool clarity needed to make tough decisions, hold boundaries, and stay focused on the larger mission even when emotions run high.

Fall too far to either side, and something breaks. Too much empathy without detachment, and you get overwhelmed, enmeshed, emotionally exhausted. Too much detachment without empathy, and you become robotic, distant, out of touch.

The art of leadership lies in the dance between the two.

8.4.1   The Empath's Dilemma

Empathy is not just a leadership skill; it's a human superpower. It connects. It calms. It motivates. But empathy can also seduce. It can lure you into trying to fix everything, feel everything, carry everything. You begin to take responsibility for emotions that aren't yours to own.

You start blurring the line between being supportive and being consumed.

This is the empath's dilemma: *How do you stay deeply human without becoming emotionally hostage to every situation?*

The answer is not to feel less. It is to feel with more awareness.

8.4.2   Detachment Is Not Disengagement

There's a misconception in leadership that detachment means being cold, aloof, or emotionally unavailable. But true operational detachment is none of these.

Detachment is not the absence of feeling; it is the anchoring of feeling so it doesn't sweep you away.

It means being able to hold space for someone's story without making it your own.

It means making a hard decision with a heavy heart, but still making it.

It means understanding that sometimes, protecting the whole means disappointing a few.

Detachment doesn't make you less compassionate. It keeps your compassion clear-eyed and effective.

8.4.3   The Inner Compass: Head and Heart in Dialogue

The most grounded leaders don't choose between empathy and detachment; they integrate them. They develop an inner compass where the heart informs the head, and the head tempers the heart.

They learn to:

Listen deeply to what people are feeling, but act based on what the situation needs.

Offer emotional support, but stay focused on the system, the structure, and the outcomes.

Care for individuals, but not compromise the collective.

Feel someone's disappointment, but not let it derail necessary progress.

This kind of balanced leadership doesn't come naturally to most. It is practiced. Refined. Learned through missteps, reflection, and self-awareness.

8.4.4   Leading With a Strong Back and a Soft Front

There's a beautiful phrase from Zen teacher Roshi Joan Halifax: *Strong back, Soft front.*

A strong back means you stand in your values, your clarity, your firmness.

A soft front means you lead with openness, humility, and compassion.

The strength keeps you from collapsing. The softness keeps you from hardening.

That's the posture of the balanced leader. Grounded enough to hold the vision. Human enough to hold the room.

8.4.5   Reflection: The Quiet Grace of Poise

Leadership isn't just about bold decisions or grand gestures. Sometimes, it's about the quiet grace of poise. It's the ability to stand steady when emotions swirl, and to stay open without being swept away.

Empathy lets you touch hearts. Detachment helps you keep yours intact.

True strength is not in choosing one over the other, but in holding both. In leading with a clear mind and a kind soul. In being compassionate without collapsing, decisive without disconnecting.

Because the best leaders are not those who feel nothing, nor those who feel everything.

They are the ones who feel enough, and know what to do with it.

CHAPTER 9

The Cost of Not Being Blamed

Escaping blame doesn't mean escaping consequence.

Avoiding blame may seem like a success, but it can carry an invisible cost. It erodes trust, credibility, and moral clarity. Leaders who artfully sidestep fault might win the moment but lose the deeper loyalty of their teams. This chapter dissects the psychology of blame avoidance and its unintended consequences, like nurturing a blame culture, diffusing courage, or diminishing long-term influence. It urges a shift from blame aversion to transparent accountability as a more powerful leadership asset, even when reputational risk is high.

9.1 How Blame Avoidance Leads to Unseen Power Shifts

9.1.1

In most systems, corporate, political, familial, even spiritual, blame is often treated like a hot potato. No one wants to hold it. It burns credibility, singes pride, and leaves behind the scent of failure. So, we pass it around or hide from it altogether. On the surface, this seems like a self-preserving instinct. But beneath it lies a quiet rearrangement of power that many never notice; until it's too late.

Blame, though uncomfortable, is a form of accountability. It's the tether that connects authority to consequence. When someone takes the fall, consciously or not, the spotlight shifts, sometimes subtly, sometimes dramatically. And when no one takes the fall? That's when things begin to unravel.

In a culture where everyone sidesteps blame, leadership doesn't disappear; it just migrates. Often, it moves toward those who are willing to shoulder the burden, even when it's not their fault. Ironically, those who refuse blame relinquish influence. Their need to protect their image ends up eroding their authority. Responsibility, real or perceived, becomes a gravitational force. People begin to orbit around those who carry the weight, not those who deflect it.

In teams, the person who quietly fixes things without making noise about blame becomes the de facto leader. In families, the emotionally resilient one often becomes the glue, not because they wanted to be, but because others stepped back. In politics, history remembers those who stood up in times of failure more than those who vanished into the fog of denial.

Blame avoidance also creates power vacuums. And nature, as we know, abhors a vacuum. When traditional leaders dodge responsibility, informal ones rise. These unofficial actors start making decisions, forming alliances, and influencing outcomes, not because they were appointed, but because they were present when things broke. Authority, like trust, flows toward those who are dependable under pressure.

There's also a dangerous kind of power that emerges here, the manipulator who thrives in blame-averse cultures. When no one wants to be blamed, the door opens for those who know how to redirect guilt, spread confusion, and stay just outside the line of fire. Over time, they gain control not through merit, but through mastery of blame deflection.

And so, what begins as a simple act of self-protection, *"Let's not talk about who's at fault"*, turns into a quiet rearrangement of influence. The power map changes. The decision-makers aren't always the ones with titles anymore. They are the ones who either step into the void or learn to navigate it with cunning.

Blame avoidance is not neutral. It has a cost, even when it feels polite or politically correct. It creates hidden hierarchies, unintended leaders, and a culture where truth bends to convenience. More crucially, it breaks the vital chain between ownership and influence, the very chain that keeps systems functional and leaders accountable.

Sometimes, the true shift in power doesn't happen at the boardroom table or the campaign rally. It happens when someone says, *"Don't look at me,"* and someone else quietly says, *"I'll fix it."*

9.1.2   Story 1: The Quiet Rise of the Project Manager

At a leading infrastructure company, a multi-crore project was slowly spiraling into chaos. The schedule was slipping, budgets were bleeding, and vendor coordination had turned into a blame game. Every meeting became a theatre of deflection. The senior leadership, eloquent, seasoned, and politically astute, were more focused on crafting narratives than fixing problems.

Each time an issue was raised, there was someone with a neatly packaged excuse.

"This delay was because the procurement team didn't clear the vendor on time."

"We missed the milestone because engineering didn't respond to the design queries fast enough."

"There's been a communication gap; someone was supposed to follow up."

No one wanted to own the problem. They wanted to own the version of the story that made them look innocent.

Amidst all this, a low-profile project manager named Archana kept working quietly. She simply carried the responsibility for a part of the work that was right at the centre of the chaos. She wasn't flashy in meetings, didn't indulge in the politics, and rarely raised her voice. But what she did do, consistently, was take responsibility.

When a supplier failed to deliver, she didn't point fingers. She called them, rescheduled deliveries, worked out late-night logistics, and made it happen. When internal teams missed deadlines, she sat with them, understood constraints, and reshuffled tasks to keep things moving.

Slowly, without a formal announcement or a new title, people started turning to her. Senior managers began asking for her opinion. Vendors bypassed official channels to coordinate with her. Even other project teams began requesting her help in solving their issues.

Within six months, Archana, who initially had no authority over the entire project, was effectively running it. Not because someone gave her the power, but because everyone else had surrendered it through blame avoidance.

The official heads remained in their seats, but the centre of influence had shifted. Quietly. Organically. Unseen.

By the time the project recovered, the leadership had to acknowledge the shift. Archana was offered a new position, not just as a reward, but as a recognition of where the real leadership had emerged.

Reflection

Blame avoidance by those in power created a void. And it was filled, not by someone louder or more politically savvy, but by someone who simply owned what others didn't. That's how unseen power shifts happen. Not with a bang, but with a quiet act of ownership.

9.1.3   Story 2: The Rise of the Invisible Puppet Master

In a large government-run utility organisation, internal politics were part of the landscape, but there was a long-standing tradition of shared ownership, until a high-profile joint-venture project with a private partner turned sour.

The project hit several early snags, cost overruns, misaligned technical specs, and delays due to conflicting work cultures. Instead of confronting these issues directly, senior leaders began dodging responsibility, fearing public backlash and loss of stature.

Enter Raj, a senior deputy with no formal authority over the JV but a keen sense of office dynamics. Raj had mastered the art of subtle influence. He never made bold decisions, never signed off on anything critical, and was never listed in project minutes as accountable for any failure.

Instead, he positioned himself as the helpful advisor. He attended every critical meeting, spoke just enough to sound informed, and always stayed just a few degrees removed from direct execution. He floated between departments, subtly suggesting what should be done, never issuing commands, but always planting ideas.

When problems escalated, Raj was quick to 'support' investigations. He offered just enough information to point fingers at others while keeping his own hands clean. He whispered to leadership about 'gaps in judgment' in other teams, and occasionally leaked incomplete data that shifted blame without proof. Meanwhile, he took no visible risks, signed no contentious documents, and made sure his name never showed up when things went wrong.

Within a year, several capable leaders who had initially taken ownership and tried to fix the problems were sidelined. The official line was 'they failed to deliver'. But those closer to the action knew they had been overwhelmed, partly by the complexity of the project, but more by the quiet sabotage and reluctance of others to support them.

Raj, on the other hand, had become indispensable. The top brass trusted him because he had 'warned them early'. He was promoted, not for delivering results, but for being politically useful in a culture that feared visible blame.

The organisation didn't realise it at first, but something had shifted; real leadership had eroded. People became afraid to take bold steps or offer honest opinions. Initiative was replaced by risk-averse silence. Ownership was replaced by blame gaming.

And Raj? He had no enemies, only pawns.

Reflection

When no one wants to be blamed, those who manipulate perception gain power. The most dangerous players are not those who fail openly, but those who succeed in the shadows by ensuring others take the fall. In places where people are more afraid of being blamed than of failing, the truth gets twisted, and leadership becomes more about putting on an act than being real.

9.1.4   Story: The Comeback of Vaidehi

Vaidehi was once a rising star in a global pharma company's regional supply chain division. Sharp, efficient, and a natural problem-solver, she led with clarity and integrity. But when a critical drug shipment failed, a delay that impacted patient trials and triggered regulatory scrutiny, her world collapsed.

Though the lapse was due to multiple systemic failures, Vaidehi took full responsibility in a tense internal meeting. *"I was the final checkpoint. I own this."* Her honesty, instead of earning respect, cost her dearly. She was demoted. Meanwhile, others who were more cautious with their words, and better at shielding themselves, remained untouched.

Hurt and humiliated, Vaidehi quietly accepted a back-end logistics role. She watched from the sidelines as a new culture took hold. People learned not to speak plainly. Documents were worded ambiguously. Ownership became a liability. The team was no longer solving problems; they were just avoiding blame.

But then, a fresh crisis struck. A global raw material shortage threw procurement into disarray. Plants were stalling, and production forecasts were failing. Teams scrambled, but fear of exposure slowed every decision.

This time, Vaidehi didn't wait for permission. She stepped into the chaos.

She reactivated old vendor networks, negotiated alternate supply routes, and pulled her former team back into the fold. She took decisions others were hesitating to make, and kept records of everything, even when the outcome was uncertain. She didn't hide behind committees. She said, *"If this fails, it's on me. But let's not let fear stop us."*

Something shifted.

People who had become numb began to re-engage. Junior team members started taking initiative again. Even senior leaders, sensing a revival of clarity and courage, began to ask Vaidehi for input, not as a subordinate, but as someone they could trust.

In three months, production resumed ahead of schedule. Vaidehi didn't just solve a logistics problem; she broke a pattern. By boldly reclaiming responsibility, she gave others permission to be brave again.

This time, leadership didn't punish her honesty. They promoted her, not just in title, but in trust.

Reflection

In a blame-averse culture, taking responsibility feels like stepping into a fire. But sometimes, that fire forges real leadership. Vaidehi's story is proof that while blame can burn, authentic ownership can rebuild. She didn't just rise again; she resurrected the team's collective courage.

9.1.5   Analysis

In organisational ecosystems, accountability is not merely about assigning fault; it is a mechanism that determines who influences decisions, who garners trust, and ultimately, who leads. When individuals or teams habitually avoid blame, even in situations where ownership is warranted, the organisation experiences a silent but significant power redistribution.

1. The Vacuum Effect: When Responsibility is Evacuated

When formal leaders disengage from uncomfortable decisions or outcomes, they unintentionally create a power vacuum. This space is often filled by:

Informal influencers who are willing to take initiative.

Process custodians who understand systems better than decision-makers.

Shadow actors who leverage ambiguity for personal gain.

This vacuum does not remain neutral; it actively shifts operational and political power to those who are either bold or cunning enough to occupy it.

2. The Rise of Informal Authority

In high-stakes environments, those who take ownership, whether or not they are formally accountable, begin to accumulate:

Credibility from peers and subordinates

Access to decision-making platforms

Trust from those who seek clarity in confusion

This phenomenon can be constructive (as seen in transformational figures like Vaidehi) or corrosive (as with individuals like Raj). In both cases, the common trigger is the retreat of formal authority from visible ownership.

3. Cultural Consequences of Blame Aversion

An organisation where blame avoidance becomes normalised exhibits the following traits:

Trait	Consequence
Decision Paralysis	Leaders delay or delegate critical calls to avoid future accountability
Documentation Theatre	Teams over-document to deflect responsibility rather than drive clarity
Political Survivorship	Those who navigate perception better than performance thrive
Initiative Attrition	High-potential employees disengage due to lack of psychological safety

This leads to an erosion of trust, stagnation in innovation, and an overall decline in moral ownership across ranks.

4. Strategic Risk: When No One Is to Blame, No One Is Leading

From a leadership strategy perspective, an organisation that fears blame more than failure is vulnerable to:

Misaligned execution - because there's no clarity on who owns outcomes.

Tactical myopia - where every short-term cover-up erodes long-term vision.

Reputation decay - as stakeholders perceive the organisation as evasive rather than accountable.

Leaders must recognise that avoiding blame is not a neutral act; it is a strategic error that invites misgovernance.

5. Restoring the Balance: Promoting Accountable Cultures

To counter this shift, organisations must re-engineer how blame and ownership are perceived. This includes:

Psychological safety audits: Do people feel safe taking responsibility?

Rewarding clarity over caution: Promote those who bring transparency, even under pressure.

Narrative framing by leadership: Leaders must openly own decisions and signal that taking responsibility is a strength, not a risk.

Decoupling blame from punishment: Especially in developmental errors, cultivate a culture where admitting fault is the first step toward improvement, not retribution.

9.1.6   Summary: Ownership Finds a Way

Even when leadership is abdicated, accountability doesn't vanish; it simply migrates.

Those who avoid blame may shield themselves in the short term, but in doing so, they surrender long-term influence. And those who step up, willingly or by necessity, inherit not just tasks, but the true levers of leadership through trust, discretion, and moral authority.

This is the paradox of inescapable ownership:

You can refuse to be blamed. You cannot refuse to be replaced.

In a blame-averse culture, the most powerful shift is often invisible; when responsibility, left unclaimed, becomes the seedbed of a new power structure.

The question for every organisation is not just who failed, but who stood up when others stepped back?

9.2   The Strategic Risk of a Blame-Free Culture

9.2.1   When Psychological Safety Becomes a Shield for Mediocrity

In recent years, organisations have rightly prioritised psychological safety; creating environments where individuals can speak up without fear of retribution. But when this noble intent mutates into an overcorrection, it gives rise to a different threat. It leads to a culture where no one is to blame for anything.

And when no one is to blame, nothing is truly owned.

At first glance, such environments appear harmonious. Meetings are civil. Reports are diplomatic. Failures are termed 'learning moments'. But beneath the surface, unresolved issues accumulate, decisions get diluted, and mediocrity finds protection under the guise of inclusivity.

1. Mistaking Safety for Absence of Consequence

A healthy culture of psychological safety encourages bold thinking and transparency.

A dysfunctional blame-free culture:

Confuses feedback with fault-finding.

Avoids difficult conversations under the pretext of respect.

Mistakes silence for alignment.

Over time, a subtle message emerges: *'It's safer to be inoffensive than to be accountable.'*

This is not safety; it is strategic stagnation.

2. The Erosion of Decision-Making Integrity

In a blame-free culture, the fear is not failure; it is visibility. *Leaders and teams:*

Opt for consensus over clarity.

Spread decisions thinly to avoid individual ownership.

Write reports that are 'technically accurate' but tactically meaningless.

Strategically, this creates organisations that move slowly, superficially, and safely; traits incompatible with high-stakes industries, innovation, or crisis management.

3. Accountability Vacuum and Organisational Drift

Without meaningful accountability:

Strategic Area	Risk in a Blame-Free Culture
Innovation	No one dares to push boundaries without cover for failure.
Customer Experience	Errors are rationalised instead of resolved.
Operational Agility	Decision loops expand as responsibility dilutes.
Leadership Development	Future leaders are trained to avoid risk, not embrace responsibility.

When no one is blamed, the real danger is that no one truly leads.

4. The Illusion of Harmony, The Reality of Rot

Blame-free cultures are often applauded for being 'healthy' and 'non-toxic'. But that appearance of harmony is sometimes an illusion; a polished surface concealing systemic avoidance. In such environments:

High performers burn out - they feel unsupported and overburdened.

Underperformers persist - rarely confronted, rarely corrected.

Culture loses its edge - compassion becomes compliance.

5. Strategic Correction: Reinventing Responsibility Without Fear

The goal is not to return to punitive blame; it is to reinstate meaningful ownership. *This requires:*

Defining what must be owned: Every key outcome should have a single point of accountability.

Making learning visible, but responsibility clearer: Celebrate lessons learned and the courage to stand up when things go wrong.

Cultivating resilient leaders: Those who are not just psychologically safe, but emotionally strong enough to carry responsibility.

Reframing feedback: Not as fault-finding, but as course correction in the pursuit of excellence.

9.2.2   How do you build a culture that is safe to fail, but not free to hide?

This idea sounds great, but living it out takes thought and effort. It means your team should feel safe to try, make mistakes, and learn, but they shouldn't be allowed to disappear, avoid responsibility, or stay silent when it matters.

Here's how leaders can make that happen:

1. Make it okay to fail, if you're trying to grow

Let your people know it's okay to try things that don't work, as long as they're learning something.

Talk about your own failures too; show them you're human.

When things go wrong, ask:

"What did we learn?" not *"Who messed up?"*

2. But don't let people hide behind silence or excuses

Make it clear who's responsible for what.

If something isn't working, people should speak up early; not wait for things to break.

Give your team regular chances to share updates, ask for help, or admit they're stuck. That way, problems don't stay hidden.

3. Create a space where people can speak up honestly

Encourage people to be direct but kind.

Build trust so people feel they can say, *"I don't know how to do this,"* or *"I think we're going the wrong way."*

And when someone gives feedback, thank them; don't punish them.

4. Focus on the problem, not the person

When something goes wrong, don't attack the individual.

Ask,

"What got in the way?" or *"What can we do differently next time?"*

Help people improve instead of making them afraid of failing again.

5. Use tools that help everyone stay honest

Keep things visible.

Use simple check-ins, shared task lists, or dashboards so everyone knows what's going on.

This isn't about spying; it's about keeping each other in the loop.

6. Promote people who take ownership, not just those who succeed

Support those who are honest, who learn quickly, and who help others grow.

These are the kind of people who make a strong, trusting culture.

A culture like this says:

"It's okay to fall; we'll help you up."

"But don't go missing when things get tough. We need you to show up, speak up, and take part."

9.2.3   Summary: Without Accountability, Strategy Becomes Sentiment

A culture without blame is not automatically a strong culture.

It can just as easily be a sentiment-driven system, where politeness masks passivity, and kindness becomes complicity.

Strategically, the absence of blame must not lead to the absence of clarity.

Leaders must build cultures where people are safe to fail, but not free to hide.

Because in the long run, an organisation that fears confrontation more than failure is one that will quietly lose its edge.

9.3   Building Systems That Reward Transparent Ownership Over Clever Escapes

In most organisations, people quickly learn that the safest path is not always the most honest one. What's rewarded is not necessarily accountability, but often the ability to appear untouchable. And so, clever escapes like shifting blame, dodging questions, or wrapping poor decisions in vague language become survival skills. The real cost? A culture where truth becomes optional, learning is stifled, and long-term trust quietly erodes.

To counter this, leaders must do more than just preach ownership. They must build systems that make it safer to be transparent than to be evasive.

9.3.1 Ownership is a Risk - Make It Worth It

By taking ownership involves risk, you're exposing your actions, your decisions, and sometimes your mistakes. If the organisational system punishes those who come forward and silently rewards those who hide behind bureaucracy, why would anyone step up?

Instead of asking why aren't people taking ownership, we should ask what happens when they do?

If the only reward is extra work, public embarrassment, or being labelled the 'fall guy', you've built a system where the clever escape becomes rational. The challenge, then, is to flip the script. Make owning up a sign of strength, not vulnerability. Make it the doorway to growth, not a trigger for punishment.

Illustration

Consider the case of Dr. E. Sreedharan, the 'Metro Man of India'. When he took charge of the Delhi Metro project, he insisted on full ownership of timelines, budgets, and delivery standards. He refused to hide behind red tape. He openly shared both progress and setbacks with stakeholders and the media. His transparent style stood in stark contrast to the usual blame-shifting culture in infrastructure projects.

And what happened? The Delhi Metro became a benchmark of project delivery in India, completed ahead of schedule and under budget. It was not just his technical skill; it was the system he built around honest reporting, swift accountability, and a deep sense of ownership.

This is ownership rewarded. And it wasn't just personal glory; it changed the perception of public transport in urban India.

9.3.2   Design for Candour, Not Just Compliance

One of the easiest traps for organisations to fall into is mistaking compliance for integrity. People tick boxes, submit reports, and go through the motions; not because they're being accountable, but because they're avoiding exposure. The system says 'you followed procedure', but nobody's asking if the decision was right, or if something could have been done better.

Transparent ownership requires psychological safety. This means creating an environment where people can speak up about what went wrong, without immediately fearing what will happen to them. It doesn't mean there are no consequences for failure, but it means the response is developmental, not punitive.

Instead of *'Who's to blame?'* the first question should be: *'What can we learn from this, and how do we prevent it next time?'*

Illustration

Let's contrast Delhi Metro project with another Illustration Indian banking. During the build-up of the Non-Performing Asset (NPA) crisis in the early 2010s, many senior executives across public sector banks refrained from calling out bad loans early. Why? Because the system punished admission of a problem more harshly than the problem itself. If a loan defaulted during your tenure, even if it originated earlier, you were held liable, regardless of your effort to recover or restructure.

So, clever escapes became the norm. Bad loans were 'evergreened' to avoid detection, repayments were rescheduled repeatedly, and reports were sugarcoated. The cost? Billions in stressed assets, erosion of trust, and years of cleanup by the taxpayer.

Now contrast that with recent reforms where prompt corrective actions and public disclosures became the norm, and newer leadership was encouraged to face the problem squarely, rather than hide it. That's the beginning of a shift; from blaming to learning.

9.3.3   Incentivising the Right Behaviour

Incentives shape culture. If the heroes in your system are those who never seem to make mistakes (or never admit them), then you've unintentionally made honesty a liability. But what if promotions, recognition, and trust were given not just for outcomes, but for the maturity of ownership displayed in pursuit of those outcomes?

Celebrate the manager who flags a strategic risk early, not the one who looks flawless until the last minute. Promote the engineer who takes responsibility for a failure and guides the team to a better solution; not the one who quietly distances themselves from it. Recognise the leader who creates space for their team to admit struggles, over the one who keeps everyone 'in line'.

Illustrations

One of India's standout stories in this regard is from Infosys, under Narayana Murthy's leadership. In the early years, Murthy made it a point to acknowledge mistakes in board meetings and encouraged his senior leadership to own up to misses. There was no space for blame games. What got rewarded was clarity, integrity, and constructive response; not evasion.

Employees were empowered to speak truth to power, report errors, and work on solutions without fear of retribution. This became part of Infosys' ethical DNA, which helped it gain global credibility long before Indian IT was seen as a global force.

Similarly, in ISRO, when missions have failed, like the Chandrayaan-2 lander crash, leadership, including then-chairman K. Sivan, addressed the nation with composure, owning the setback and focusing on what could be learned. Not a single junior scientist was scapegoated. And just four years later, ISRO delivered Chandrayaan-3's success, thanks to that very learning culture.

This is what happens when a system encourages 'fail forward' ownership, rather than clever evasion.

9.3.4   Escaping Clever Escapes

It's tempting to admire someone who always seems to sidestep blame. But when that cleverness becomes an organisational norm, it breeds mediocrity. People become skilled at hiding, spinning, and deflecting, until something breaks, and then everyone wonders what happened.

Instead of admiring the political survivor, organisations must start admiring the courageous contributor; the one who owns their space, speaks their truth, and helps fix what's broken. These are the people who build cultures of trust, innovation, and long-term excellence.

Illustration

One promising case is the Direct Benefit Transfer (DBT) system in welfare schemes. Earlier, leakages in subsidy delivery were routinely swept under the rug by blaming intermediaries. But when bureaucrats like Nandan Nilekani, working with the government, owned the responsibility to make Aadhaar-linked transfers work transparently, they invited scrutiny, criticism, and technical obstacles, but they stood firm. The result? Tens of thousands of Crores saved from ghost beneficiaries. Ownership led to systemic change.

The old clever escape, 'the system is too big to fix', was abandoned.

9.3.5   In Summary

Clever escapes may win the moment, but transparent ownership builds legacy.

It's up to leaders to tilt the system. Build rewards around truth, not performance theatre. Protect those who speak up. Promote those who take full responsibility for their work, flaws and all. And always remember, what gets rewarded will be repeated.

True excellence doesn't come from avoiding blame. It comes from a shared commitment to face it, and grow beyond it.

9.4   *Case Study: When Organisational Systems Enable Optics Over Ownership*

This is a case of clever and cunning escape from blame. It's an organisational trick where optics triumphed over ownership. Beneath the veneer of progress, a pattern of systematic misrepresentation unfolded, artfully orchestrated by those in power and silently sanctioned by the very systems meant to uphold accountability. Rather than being anomalies, these deceptive practices became the norm, camouflaged as performance and rewarded as achievement. What emerges is not an isolated lapse, but a culture that honed the art of escaping responsibility while appearing to deliver results. Here is a telling example of how an organisation can institutionalise evasion under the guise of success.

Context

In a project-based organisation with multi-year gestation periods, project planning and monitoring functions reported directly to the respective Project Heads. These Project Heads, across the board, consistently reported inflated progress figures, both physical and financial, to meet targets and secure performance-based incentives. This behaviour was not isolated but deeply ingrained in the organisational culture.

Observed Practices

1. **End-of-Year Frenzy and Recurrent Underperformance:** As financial year-ends approached, teams were pressured to meet projected milestones, leading to last-minute reporting activity that often overstated actual achievements. Inevitably, this would result in underperformance being reported later, but by then, the immediate benefits, particularly incentives, had already been claimed.

2. **Systematic Inflation of Progress for Incentives:** Project Heads, many of whom were nearing superannuation, would deliberately inflate progress figures to become eligible for performance-linked rewards. Their successors, upon assuming charge, would conduct a realistic assessment and report much lower actual progress, leading to a formal reset of targets. This cycle repeated itself across projects and timeframes.

3. **Absence of Internal Accountability:** Despite repeated instances of project delays and cost overruns, internal accountability was conspicuously absent. Deviations were routinely attributed to delays in finalisation of drawings, a reason conveniently aligned with the telescopic nature of design finalisation in such projects. This explanation, although partially valid, was routinely used as a blanket justification.

4. **Leadership Complicity:** Even at the highest levels of leadership, including the CEO, there was little resistance to this practice. Since the system of inflated reporting benefitted multiple tiers of leadership by enabling them to claim performance incentives, corrective interventions were either absent or actively discouraged.

5. **Rejection of Transparent Systems:** A notable suggestion to implement SAP's project monitoring tools, capable of tracking true financial and physical progress, was ignored. Such systems, which could have introduced objectivity and accountability, were perceived as threats to the prevailing culture of inflated reporting and were thus sidelined.

Analysis: System Failure in Rewarding Transparent Ownership

This case highlights a systemic failure to build mechanisms that reward transparent ownership. Instead, it promoted an environment that incentivised short-term, self-serving behaviours disguised as performance.

1. **Perverse Incentive Structures:** Tying incentives to reported progress without adequate validation mechanisms encouraged misrepresentation.

2. **Lack of Cross-Tenure Accountability:** Retiring leaders had no accountability for the consequences of misreported progress, passing the burden onto successors who had to 'rebase' expectations.

3. **Cultural Reinforcement of Evasion:** With no checks from internal stakeholders and widespread complicity, the culture became one of clever escape rather than authentic delivery.

4. **Neglect of Systemic Tools:** Transparency tools such as SAP were resisted, not because of inefficiency, but because they threatened the status quo.

Strategic Reflections: How to Flip the System

To move from rewarding clever escapes to rewarding transparent ownership, systems must be redesigned with the following principles:

1. Make Progress Verifiable and Continuously Audited

Use immutable systems like SAP or digital project trackers with auto-audits.

Ensure milestones are evidence-backed, not declaration-based.

2. Align Incentives to Long-Term Outcomes

Delay full incentive release until project milestones sustain over time.

Tie retiring leaders' incentives to independent verification of progress by successors.

3. Establish Shared Accountability, Not Siloed Blame

Introduce cross-functional oversight panels.

Institutionalise knowledge transfer and audit between outgoing and incoming leaders.

4. Encourage Cultural Whistle-blowing with Protection

Build safe channels to call out reporting manipulation.

Reward truth-tellers, not report-polishers.

A Leadership Lesson

A leader once said, *"Culture is not what you preach. It's what you tolerate."*

This story is not just about manipulation; it's about systemic tolerance for cleverness at the cost of truth.

Transparent ownership requires courage, systems, and a cultural reset. Until the incentives reward honesty over optics, clever escapes will thrive.

CHAPTER 10

Inherited Responsibility: Leading Amid Legacy Decisions

You didn't choose it, but it chose you.

Leaders often step into roles laden with unresolved tensions, outdated systems, and decisions made long before their tenure began. Though they didn't architect the past, they are tasked with its consequences. This chapter explores the nuanced challenge of inherited responsibility, the paradox of being held answerable for choices you never made. It offers insights on navigating legacy issues with wisdom; how to honour institutional memory while steering toward necessary reinvention, and how to hold ownership without resentment or victimhood.

10.1 Taking Charge of Ghosts: Leading Within Decisions You Didn't Make

10.1.1

There is a quiet discomfort that comes with inheriting decisions you didn't make. It's the feeling of walking into a room after the lights have been switched off, trying to make sense of the silhouettes. You weren't in the room when the decisions were made, but now you live with their consequences, and more importantly, you are expected to lead through them.

These are the ghosts left behind by past leadership. They include strategies that stopped working long ago, promises that were never fully kept, outdated systems still hanging around, and unspoken agreements people quietly follow without question. You didn't author these choices, but they now reside in your domain, quietly shaping the culture, processes, and even the morale of your team. As a leader, you inherit not just the role but the residue of what came before.

Many leaders instinctively want to draw a line: *'That wasn't my decision'*, they'll say. *'This happened before my time'*. It gets in the way of what leadership truly calls for, which is taking responsibility. Whether or not the decision was yours, the fallout is. The team doesn't care about who made the call; they care about who will steer them through it. That's you.

Taking charge of ghosts is not about blaming the past. Nor is it about blindly defending it. It's about acknowledging that the past is now your starting point, not your excuse.

You may inherit a team burned out by an old restructuring. Or a product roadmap weighed down by unrealistic past expectations. You might find yourself leading with limited resources because of budget decisions made years ago in a different reality. These are not just 'challenges'. They are inherited contexts, and how you engage with them defines your credibility.

One of the most difficult aspects of inherited responsibility is emotional leadership. People carry memories. They remember promises made and broken. They remember times when they weren't heard. They might be cynical, defensive, or simply tired. And now, you walk in with a clean slate, but to them, you are the continuation of a story they're still living. The onus is on you to write the next chapter in a way that helps them believe again.

So, how do you lead when you're walking through someone else's shadow?

First, seek understanding, not just data. What were the intentions behind those old decisions? Were they misguided, or were they right for a different time? Understanding the 'why' doesn't excuse poor outcomes, but it can shape wiser responses. The past becomes a teacher, not a villain.

Second, own the now. While you may not be responsible for the situation, you are responsible within it. That subtle shift in mindset is powerful. It transforms you from a passive inheritor into an active steward. Leaders don't just clean up messes; they restore confidence in the future.

Third, decide what to honour and what to shed. Not all legacy decisions are wrong, some are simply outdated. Others were wise but miscommunicated. Distinguish between what deserves continuation, what needs reimagining, and what must be gracefully retired. This is where leadership becomes craftsmanship.

Finally, speak with honesty and hope. Your team doesn't expect magic, but they crave clarity. Let them know you see the ghosts. That you're not pretending they don't exist. But also let them know you believe in something better. Legacy does not define destiny; our leadership does.

Taking charge of ghosts is one of the quietest, hardest things leaders do. There's no glory in it, no applause. But it's what transforms a manager into a leader. It's what allows trust to be rebuilt. And sometimes, it's what finally sets a whole organisation free.

10.1.2   Case Study: A real and heartbreaking example

In a very old housing society, the buildings had grown dilapidated and were eventually demolished in preparation for redevelopment. But what should have been the beginning of a new chapter turned into a decade-long nightmare. The current leadership, the new Secretary of the society, wasn't responsible for what had happened decades ago. But now, they are living with the ghosts of past decisions.

The boundary walls had been constructed in violation of the original approved plan. Over time, neighbouring societies took quiet, illegal possession of the land that belonged to this housing society. FSI (Floor Space Index), the precious developmental right of the society, was neither tracked nor safeguarded. Opportunistic neighbours, sensing the lapse, falsified documents and appropriated the society's rightful FSI.

It didn't stop there. The previous managing committees, perhaps ignorant of legal implications or driven by short-term pressures, sold parts of the common built-up area, something never meant to be commodified. Other issues were ignored, buried, or forgotten. And when the time for redevelopment came, these ghosts returned, each one dragging the society into legal tangles and bureaucratic impasses.

The buildings were already gone. But the members, many elderly or financially stretched, found themselves paying EMIs for homes that no longer existed, and rent for the ones they now lived in. Hope, for many, had turned into a financial and emotional burden.

Into this storm walked the new Secretary.

He didn't make these decisions. He didn't approve the flawed plans, sell the spaces, or let the FSI slip through the cracks. But he has inherited the fallout. He now battles fraudulent neighbours, government machinery, and a litigious maze. He absorbs the frustrations of members who feel betrayed, while fighting for a future that seems endlessly deferred. The toll is immense. It affects you physically, mentally, and emotionally.

This is what taking charge of ghosts looks like.

And it brings us to the essence of inherited responsibility in leadership. It's not about blame; it's about the burden. And how you carry it determines whether you perpetuate the problem or begin the healing.

Here are a few principles that can guide leaders through such inherited turmoil:

1. Understand the 'Why' Behind the Ghosts

Legacy issues often have deeper roots. They can come from ignorance, missing systems, or tough choices people had to make just to get by in earlier times. The past, though flawed, is rarely born of pure malice. In this housing society's case, earlier committees may have lacked legal literacy, were misinformed, or failed to foresee the implications of neglect. Understanding the intent behind past decisions can open a path to repair, not resentment.

2. Own the Present, Even If You Didn't Create the Past

When you inherit chaos, your power lies in what you do next. The current Secretary could have disclaimed responsibility, but leadership demands more. His choice to confront, fight, and persist, even under strain, is what transforms stewardship into courage. Whether or not you caused the mess, leading through it requires full emotional and operational ownership.

3. Communicate With Radical Transparency

Members in the society are not just victims of bad past decisions; they're anxious, confused, and losing faith. Leaders dealing with inherited issues must not pretend to 'have it under control' when they don't. Honest, empathetic communication can be an antidote to cynicism. It's not about giving easy answers, but about giving people reason to believe the journey is worth continuing.

4. Rebuild With Wisdom, Not Revenge

When old neighbours cheat you, or past decisions seem criminally negligent, it's tempting to respond with rage. But strategic rebuilding is different from emotional retaliation. The Secretary must pick legal battles wisely, push systemic reforms, and seek sustainable, lawful solutions. Revenge may feel righteous, but only wisdom repairs.

5. Find Support Before You Burn Out

No one can carry ghosts alone. Whether it's legal allies, empathetic members, or even mental health support, inherited leadership crises demand shared strength. The Secretary's emotional toll must not become another ghost that haunts the future of the society. Leadership is human; its limits must be respected.

In the end, taking charge of ghosts is not about undoing the past. That's often impossible. It's about reclaiming the future, inch by inch, despite it.

Every leader, at some point, inherits consequences they did not cause. And in those moments, we're tested, not by what we built, but by what we're willing to rebuild.

And that's where true leadership begins.

10.2   *Navigating the Ethics of Historical Baggage in Institutions*

Every institution, whether corporate, governmental, academic, or social, carries within it the residue of choices made long ago. Policies etched into manuals, structures frozen in time, cultures forged under entirely different realities; these form a kind of institutional DNA. When a leader steps in, they inherit not just the authority to lead but also the weight of this legacy. Some of it is noble, even inspiring. But some of it, quietly buried, conveniently overlooked, or fiercely defended, can be deeply problematic. And then the question arises: *what do we do with our historical baggage?*

This is not merely a question of strategy; it is a profoundly ethical one. To lead well in such situations, we must learn to respect the past without avoiding hard truths, follow tradition without getting stuck in old ways, and be loyal without blindly following everything.

10.2.1 The Dilemma of Ethical Inheritance

You may find yourself leading an organisation that once engaged in practices that would now be deemed unethical; whether it was environmental negligence, discriminatory hiring, exploitation of labour, or aligning with oppressive systems. These may have occurred under 'different times,' and you may not have had any personal hand in them. And yet, here you are, wearing the badge of leadership, while history knocks gently (or sometimes loudly) at your door.

The ethical dilemma is twofold:

First, how much moral responsibility does a current leader bear for past decisions?

And second, how should they act, especially when acknowledging those decisions could mean unsettling stakeholders, reputations, or even foundational myths of the institution?

There is no universal answer. But one principle holds true; ethical clarity requires moral courage.

10.2.2 Truth Before Comfort

Choosing to confront uncomfortable histories is not a weakness; it is an act of integrity. Ethical leadership demands that we resist the temptation to paper over the past with public relations gloss or selective memory. It means engaging in open dialogues, owning up to mistakes, and initiating change, not as a performative gesture but as a sincere commitment to doing better.

Consider organisations that have issued apologies for historical injustices, revamped long-standing practices, or taken symbolic and structural actions to reconcile with communities harmed in the past. These are difficult, sometimes controversial steps. But they also represent a willingness to prioritise conscience over convenience.

10.2.3   When Legacy and Values Clash

Sometimes the inherited culture of an institution stands in direct opposition to the values you wish to champion. You may find embedded biases, opaque power structures, or traditions that resist scrutiny. Here, ethics becomes a compass, not just for what you should do, but also for how you do it.

Do you bulldoze over legacy in the name of reform? Or do you engage patiently with it, unraveling harmful threads without destroying the entire fabric? The latter path is often slower, but it builds collective ownership of change, not just compliance.

10.2.4   The Leader as Ethical Archaeologist

Leaders navigating historical baggage must become a kind of ethical archaeologist. They have to dig deep, sift carefully, understand the context, and interpret the findings with wisdom. They must ask:

What part of our legacy no longer serves us, or worse, harms us?

What can we honour, without clinging blindly?

How do we differentiate between what we inherited and what we now choose to perpetuate?

And finally, the hardest one: What are we now responsible for, because we know better?

10.2.5   Moving from Guilt to Accountability

It's important to acknowledge that responsibility doesn't always imply guilt. Guilt immobilises. Responsibility empowers. You may not be guilty of what was done before your time, but now that you know, now that you lead, you are accountable for what happens next.

This is where ethical leadership becomes transformative. Not only do you steer the ship forward; you also redirect the current so that future leaders inherit something better, lighter, and more honest than what you were given.

10.2.6   Case Study: Ethics in the Eye of the Storm (continued from 10.1.2)

When we last left the story of the housing society, the new Secretary stood amid wreckage not of his making, caught between the heavy hand of history and the desperate hopes of the present. What makes his case so significant is not just the scale of inherited dysfunction, but how he chose to navigate it, with ethics as his compass, even when it cost him dearly.

Despite being under immense pressure, from members, from legal complexities, from his own crumbling health, the Secretary refused to take shortcuts. He fought quietly but resolutely in courtrooms and government corridors. With a steely mix of patience and persistence, he reclaimed the society's original FSI, the very asset that had been quietly stolen under previous regimes.

But his leadership was not confined to legal victories alone. He ensured that the ethical process was visible, inclusive, and transparent. Every major decision was placed before the members. He didn't hide behind technicalities. He didn't trade integrity for convenience. This wasn't damage control; it was value-driven reconstruction.

And yet, it came at a cost. The toll on his health, both physical and mental, cannot be overlooked. The fight for justice and rectification drained him. But he never breached ethical boundaries, nor did he let the ghosts of past decisions dictate the values of the future.

Advice: Leading with Ethics in Legacy-Chained Institutions

What can other leaders, especially those inheriting institutions with murky pasts, learn from this?

1. Let Ethics Be Your North Star, Not Expedience

When institutions are tethered to flawed legacies, it's tempting to use the same methods that caused the mess to fix it. People might shortcut the system, ignore inconvenient truths, or win at any cost. But leadership, especially in inherited crises, is not just about getting results. It's about how you get them. The Secretary didn't just recover the FSI; he recovered it ethically. And that's what gives his leadership moral legitimacy.

2. Transparency is Not a Burden, It's a Bridge

He chose regular communication over silent decision-making. Involving members in the process not only built trust; it distributed emotional ownership. When people feel they're part of the struggle, they stop pointing fingers and start joining hands.

3. Ethics Is Lonely - But It Is Not Isolated

The road of ethical leadership is often solitary, especially when others urge you to 'just fix it fast'. But solitude is not the same as isolation. Leaders must build alliances, with legal experts, moral sounding boards, empathetic team members, and sometimes, professional help. The

Secretary's health struggles remind us that ethics must not come at the cost of the self.

4. You Don't Just Inherit Problems - You Inherit the Opportunity to Heal

This case shows us that ethical leadership in legacy-bound institutions isn't just about surviving old mistakes. It's about redeeming the institution, restoring its credibility, its fairness, its future. Ethics gives you the strength to say: *We may have failed back then, but we will not fail now.*

5. Document the Journey - for Future Leaders

One of the greatest services a leader can offer is not just correction, but codification. Institutional memory tends to be short and selective. Leaders who handle legacy crises with integrity should keep a clear record of what they did, why they did it, and what they learned. Your experience can guide others and light the way forward.

In this world of broken legacies, leadership is rarely about writing on a blank slate. It is more often about writing the future over the scars of the past. The Secretary's story is not just a cautionary tale; it's a template for ethical reconstruction.

He didn't just lead the society through legal entanglements. He showed what it means to lead through moral clarity. To fight not just for a building, but for the soul of an institution.

10.3   Rewriting Inherited Narratives Without Scapegoating the Past

In leadership, we often find ourselves holding the pen of the present while reading from a script we did not write. The decisions of those before us, sometimes wise, sometimes flawed, form the backdrop against which we must act. These inherited narratives, whether cultural, organisational, or historical, can feel like both a foundation and a trap. They shape the rules we play by, the assumptions we inherit, and even the blind spots we carry.

But here's the paradox: while we are not the authors of the past, we are responsible for the present it created. The question is not whether the past was perfect; it rarely is. The real question is how we engage with it today. Do we allow the past to be our excuse, our scapegoat? Or do we choose to carry the story forward with clarity, compassion, and a commitment to do better?

Scapegoating the past is easy. It creates a clear villain and a comforting distance between 'us' and 'them'. *"They made those choices." "They set us on this path." "They didn't know better."* This instinct, while psychologically soothing, is strategically corrosive. It cultivates resentment, discourages learning, and diminishes our agency. More dangerously, it erodes trust. Internally within teams, and externally with stakeholders people can sense when leaders are more focused on deflection than direction.

True leadership means facing legacy decisions without hiding behind them. It means being honest about what happened before, without making it seem better or worse than it was. It means distinguishing between accountability and blame. Past leaders made choices in their own context, under pressures we may never fully understand. To demonise them is to flatten complexity and to miss an opportunity for growth.

Instead, rewriting the inherited narrative requires three conscious shifts:

1. From Judgment to Understanding

Understanding is not the same as approval. It means being willing to explore why things were done a certain way. To look at the constraints, fears, hopes, or beliefs that shaped those decisions. This doesn't excuse the outcomes, but it humanises the story. It enables us to extract lessons rather than launch indictments.

2. From Legacy as Burden to Legacy as Material

Inheriting something imperfect isn't a curse; it's a chance to sculpt. Leaders who see legacy decisions as raw material rather than final verdicts become alchemists of change. They build on what worked, gently dismantle what doesn't, and preserve the wisdom embedded in past intentions.

3. From Retrospective Blame to Forward Accountability

Leaders must own the future, not just manage the past. That means saying, *"Yes, this is what I've inherited, but this is where I'm taking it."* When we communicate this forward intent with transparency and humility, we invite others into a narrative of hope, not grievance.

A leader's role is not to be the historian or the one who blames the past. It is to be the aware storyteller of the ongoing journey, respecting its chapters, making changes when needed, and moving the story forward with courage.

Leading through past decisions is like walking on a narrow bridge. We are thankful for the foundation laid before us, aware of the cracks beneath us, and focussed on building a stronger path forward. Because the story doesn't end with what we inherited. It begins with what we choose to become.

CHAPTER 11

The Leadership Trap of 'Fixing Everything'

Responsibility doesn't mean omnipotence.

Driven leaders often equate responsibility with intervention, leaping into every gap, solving every problem, and assuming that ownership means omnipresence. But in doing so, they can disempower others, overextend themselves, and inadvertently become the bottleneck. This chapter investigates the 'fixer' mentality and the trap of heroic leadership. It offers models for discerning when stepping back is the more responsible act, empowering teams not by doing their work, but by trusting them to rise.

11.1 The Savior Complex in Executives

There's a moment in every executive's journey where they feel indispensable. Not just important, but absolutely central, almost divine. The belief creeps in quietly and seductively: *"If I don't step in, things will fall apart"*. And before long, they're not just leading the organisation; they're trying to save it.

This is the Savior Complex. And while it may come from a place of care, competence, or even past success, it can become a trap with steep costs.

11.1.1 The Burden of Being the Fixer

Executives who develop the Savior Complex often pride themselves on being problem-solvers. Their identity is forged in the fires of crisis management, hard decisions, and 'pulling rabbits out of hats'. But over time, what starts as a strength becomes a compulsion. They begin to see every problem as theirs to fix. Every drop in performance, every missed target, every interpersonal conflict; they own it all.

They don't delegate because they can do it faster. They don't empower because they don't trust others to do it right. And they don't step back because they've come to believe that stepping back is equivalent to abandonment.

The irony? Their need to be the savior often makes them the bottleneck.

11.1.2   When Helping Hurts

What's easy to overlook is the damage this does to the people around them. Teams that are constantly 'rescued' stop developing their own problem-solving muscles. Initiative dies. Accountability fades. And slowly, an entire culture forms where the default answer is: *'Let's wait for the boss'*.

This isn't leadership; it's learned helplessness, reinforced by a well-meaning but overreaching hand.

Even worse, the savior mindset often leads to burnout. Not just for the executive, but for everyone. The leader is overwhelmed, running on adrenaline and responsibility, but the team is disengaged, underutilised, and unmotivated. The organisation becomes dependent on a single node, which is the very antithesis of sustainable leadership.

11.1.3   The Ego Underneath

Sometimes, the Savior Complex isn't just about helping; it's about feeling needed. The executive becomes addicted to being the person who swoops in, the one who knows best, the one who always has the answers.

There's a quiet thrill in being essential. But there's also a quiet fear: *What if I'm not needed anymore?*

True leadership requires confronting that fear. It means replacing the ego-boost of fixing with the maturity of enabling. It's the difference between being the hero of the story and being the one who writes the story others get to lead.

11.1.4   Stepping Away to Truly Lead

Breaking free from the Savior Complex isn't about apathy or detachment. It's about learning to trust. Trusting that others can rise. Trusting that mistakes are part of growth. Trusting that your legacy is not built on how much you did, but on how much you empowered.

The paradox is this: when leaders stop trying to fix everything, more things actually get fixed. Because people start taking ownership. They feel trusted. And they begin to lead in their own right.

The best executives are not saviors; they're gardeners. They create conditions for others to grow. They water when needed, prune when necessary, and know when to simply step back and let nature do its work.

Because leadership isn't about saving the day. It's about building a day that no longer needs saving.

11.1.5   Story: Legacy vs. Control

In a well-established family-run FMCG business based in Maharashtra, the founder, let's call him Mr. Deshpande, was known for building the company from humble beginnings. Starting with a single unit producing traditional food items and packaged condiments, he grew it into a regional brand stocked in thousands of *kirana* stores. His decisions were legendary, his discipline unmatched, and his involvement absolute.

Even after his daughter and son returned from business schools with fresh ideas and global exposure, Mr. Deshpande remained the final word on everything. He oversaw supplier negotiations, reviewed marketing campaigns, and even approved packaging designs. Employees would often say, *"Sir ke bina kuch hota hi nahi."*

But over time, cracks began to appear. Middle management stopped taking initiative. Younger talent got frustrated. Plans for e-commerce, digital branding, and product diversification were indefinitely 'under review'.

Then came COVID.

Being in the food essentials sector, the company was allowed to continue operations with restrictions. But supply chains were disrupted, consumer behaviours changed overnight, and digital channels became critical. Physical visits were no longer viable, and agility became the new currency.

Mr. Deshpande was forced to step back. His children took charge of daily decisions, introduced e-inventory systems, activated D2C (direct-to-consumer) platforms, and streamlined backend logistics. Sales held steady, even grew, in a time of uncertainty.

Eventually, the patriarch saw the shift; the business no longer needed saving. It needed space. He shared in a team video call later, *"I thought I was shielding the company from risk. But I was also shielding it from evolution."*

11.1.6   From Savior to Enabler: The Leadership Shift That Sustains

When you catch yourself saying, *"Only I can fix this,"* pause and ask instead:

"How can I help someone else learn to fix this?"

That's the pivot, from being the solution to creating solvers.

Here's how executives can begin the shift:

1. **Audit Your Interventions:** Track where you frequently step in. Are you rescuing, or are you mentoring? If your presence is always 'necessary,' you might be the reason it is.

2. **Redefine Ownership:** Empower others by assigning full ownership, not just of tasks, but of outcomes. Support them, but don't steal the reins at the first wobble.

3. **Celebrate Process, Not Just Results:** Instead of just rewarding the right answer, reward the right approach. Did someone show initiative, even if they stumbled? That's progress worth applauding.

4. **Get Comfortable With Discomfort:** Watching others struggle can be painful, but it's where growth happens. Your silence might be the space they need to speak up and step up.

5. **Ask, Don't Tell:** Shift from giving answers to asking powerful questions. *"What options have you explored?"* invites thinking. *"Do this"* shuts it down.

11.1.7   The Enabler

Steve Jobs emphasised the importance of allowing his team members to learn from their mistakes without immediate intervention. In a discussion about managing people, he highlighted that hiring smart individuals means trusting them to navigate challenges and innovate independently. He believed that rather than dictating solutions, leaders should provide vision and allow their teams to determine the best paths forward. This approach cultivates a culture of accountability and creativity.

(Ref: Video Clip of Steve Jobs - https://youtu.be/UF8uR6Z6KLc)

11.2   *When Fixing Breaks More Than It Repairs*

Leaders often wear their problem-solving abilities as a badge of honour. They are praised, promoted, and respected for their decisiveness, their ability to intervene swiftly, and for their instinct to "fix things." But under this praised instinct, there is a hidden risk. It's a quiet trap that slowly weakens the very system you're trying to fix.

The truth is, not every problem is yours to fix. And more importantly, not every intervention leads to improvement.

In fact, some of the most well-intentioned fixes, especially when done repeatedly, reactively, or unilaterally, end up creating more damage than the original problem. Like overprescribing antibiotics for a minor infection, the quick fix can weaken the organism it's trying to protect. Systems become dependent, people become disempowered, and the natural process of learning through challenge is short-circuited.

This is the paradox: the more a leader steps in to fix, the more fragile the environment becomes.

11.2.1   The Subtle Erosion of Ownership

When a leader is always ready to jump in and solve, others eventually stop trying. Not because they're incapable, but because they've learned that their efforts will be overridden or corrected anyway. Over time, initiative dries up, problem-solving muscles atrophy, and a quiet culture of passivity takes root.

The organisation becomes like a bike with training wheels that were never meant to come off, safe, stable, but permanently limited in speed and agility.

What starts as care turns into control.

What begins as support ends as suppression.

11.2.2   Mistaking Symptoms for Root Causes

Another reason fixing backfires is because leaders are often exposed to symptoms, not root causes. And when one responds too quickly to surface-level issues, one risks reinforcing deeper dysfunctions.

For example, a team consistently missing deadlines might seem to call for stricter monitoring or better time management tools. But what if the real issue is unclear priorities, a lack of psychological safety, or misaligned incentives? By treating the symptom, the leader inadvertently protects the dysfunction, allowing it to fester quietly beneath the surface.

True leadership sometimes requires not reacting, at least not immediately. It demands curiosity before conclusion.

11.2.3   The Emotional Toll of Over-Fixing

There's also the emotional wear and tear. Leaders who feel they must always step in eventually burn out. They become exhausted, resentful, or cynical, not because others failed, but because they never allowed others to grow. Fixing becomes a compulsion rather than a choice. And like all compulsions, it becomes self-defeating.

This often leads to a breakdown in relationships. Team members may start to feel infantilised or distrusted. The leader, meanwhile, may feel unappreciated or misunderstood, stuck in the lonely middle ground between saviour and scapegoat.

11.2.4   Learning to Hold the Space

Sometimes, the most powerful thing a leader can do is hold the space for others to fix the problem themselves. This isn't neglect. It's trust in action. It means resisting the urge to immediately solve, and instead asking: *"What do you think needs to be done?"* or *"How might we explore this together?"*

It means enduring the discomfort of silence, ambiguity, or temporary failure so that more durable, meaningful solutions can emerge.

Leadership is not about having all the answers. It's about creating the conditions where others can find their own.

11.2.5   Illustration: The PSU Chairman and the Maintenance Maze

A few years ago, the chairman of a major Indian Public Sector Undertaking in the energy sector noticed a rising trend in equipment failure reports from a particular region. The regional head and his team, aware of the chairman's hands-on style, sent daily updates and pleaded for immediate support. Seeing the urgency, the chairman set up a special task force from the head office, which flew down, investigated, and implemented a 'fix' by issuing standardised preventive maintenance checklists and sending technical supervisors for compliance.

Initially, it looked like a success. Breakdowns fell. Reports became neat. The chairman was satisfied.

But six months later, the failures returned with a vengeance. This time, even minor technical issues escalated into major shutdowns. Investigations revealed a subtle truth; the regional teams had stopped thinking. They were simply following checklists, waiting for instructions, and escalating problems. Field-level ingenuity, a key trait in managing India's diverse and often unpredictable operating environments, had vanished.

What broke the system wasn't bad leadership. It was over-leadership. The central intervention unintentionally stripped ownership from the people who knew the ground reality best. The real issue wasn't the absence of SOPs; it was the absence of trust in the field's ability to diagnose and adapt.

11.2.6   Empower Before You Intervene

Audience: "What is the most important thing you learned at Apple that you are doing it NexT?"

Steve Jobs: "I am not sure I learned this when I was at Apple, but I learned it based on the data when I was at Apple. And that is, I now take a longer term view on people. In other words when I see something not being done right, my first isn't to go and fix it, it's to say we are building a team here and we're going to great stuff for the next decade, not just for the next year. And so what do I need to do to help so that the person screwing up learns"

(Ref.: Video Clip of Steve Jobs - https://www.facebook.com/reel/ 464588212779950 *)*

11.3   Creating Space for Others to Step in, Without Abdicating

11.3.1

One of the quietest forms of leadership is knowing when not to act. It's the discipline of stepping back, not to escape responsibility, but to make room for others to rise. It's counterintuitive, especially for high-performing leaders whose instincts are tuned to spot problems and solve them before they fester. But leadership is not just about solving; it's about building problem-solvers.

When leaders swoop in to fix everything, they unintentionally become bottlenecks. They signal to the team, "I don't trust you to figure this out", even if those words are never said. Over time, this cultivates learned helplessness; a condition where the team stops trying, assuming the leader will eventually take over anyway. Initiative withers. Ownership shrinks. And ironically, the leader becomes the very obstacle to the collective excellence they strive to enable.

Yet swinging to the other extreme, choosing to abdicate, is no better. Leaders who remove themselves entirely under the guise of empowerment can breed confusion and drift. Without support, people feel abandoned. *The paradox lies in striking the delicate balance:* creating space without creating a vacuum.

So, what does this balance look like in practice?

It means staying close enough to care, but far enough to not interfere. It means setting clear expectations, being accessible, but resisting the urge to rescue. It's the art of supportive distance, where people know they're trusted, but also know you're around if things truly go off the rails.

It also means reframing your role, not as the firefighter, but as the builder of fire stations. You create systems, mindsets, and trust cultures where others are equipped to respond, reflect, and learn.

Sometimes, the greatest contribution a leader can make is silence, not because they have nothing to say, but because they choose not to rob others of the struggle that will shape them.

And yes, there will be messes. Mistakes. Things done differently than you would've done. But if everything continues to be done your way, then your leadership hasn't created capacity; it's only cloned control.

The mature leader doesn't measure success by how often they step in, but by how rarely they need to. Not because they're passive, but because they've built a team that's active.

In the end, the question is not, *"Can you fix it?"* It's, *"Can they grow by trying?"*

And if you're brave enough, sometimes the best answer… is to wait.

11.3.2   Illustration: ISRO's Silent Hand

During the Chandrayaan-2 mission, when the Vikram lander lost contact just minutes before touchdown, the world watched in stunned silence. What many didn't notice was how Dr. K. Sivan, then ISRO Chairman, handled the aftermath, not with blame or grandstanding, but by stepping back and allowing his young team of scientists and engineers to debrief, learn, and lead the future course.

Instead of taking over or shielding them from criticism, he stayed present but didn't dominate the narrative. That posture of quiet support, without micromanagement, gave birth to Chandrayaan-3, a success driven not just by better technology, but by a more empowered team. His choice to not fix everything himself gave others the courage to take ownership.

11.4   *The SPACE Framework: Creating Room Without Losing Responsibility*

Leadership is not about doing more. It's about enabling more. The greatest leaders know when to create space for others. To let them think, act, and grow. But how do you do that without slipping into passivity or detachment?

Here's a practical model to remember: S.P.A.C.E.

Each letter stands for a key principle to help leaders create room for others without letting go of accountability.

S – Set the Stage Clearly

Define the why, what, and by when.

Set the context, outcomes, and boundaries, but don't dictate the process.

Clarity is not control; it's the foundation for empowered action.

P – Provide Support, Not Solutions

Be available as a sounding board, not as a fixer.

Ask questions instead of giving instructions. Offer guidance, not direction.

Support doesn't mean solving, it means being findable and dependable.

A – Allow for Imperfection

Let people make decisions, even wrong ones. That's where learning lives.

Resist the urge to *"just do it yourself"* because it's faster or neater.

Growth often wears the mask of messiness. Honour the process.

C – Communicate Trust Proactively

Trust is not passive. It needs to be expressed.

Say it aloud: *"I trust your judgement."* It invites people to step up and think like owners.

Silence is not always golden; it can be interpreted as doubt.

E – Evaluate and Encourage Growth

Don't just assess outcomes. Reflect on ownership, initiative, and what was learned along the way.

Celebrate courage. Debrief constructively. Show you're noticing the stretch, not just the success.

Accountability is not about blame; it's about building future readiness.

Takeaway

When leaders create SPACE, they shift from being the centre of action to the creator of capacity. They resist the ego-satisfaction of solving everything and choose the deeper impact of enabling others to solve anything.

This isn't inaction. It's about creating space on purpose. It's a leadership action that is just as challenging and honorable as any decision made on the battlefield.

After all, if your leadership leaves no room for others to rise... what legacy are you truly building?

CHAPTER 12

The Ownership Echo: How Leadership Decisions Outlive You

Even after you're gone, your decisions speak.

Some decisions continue to reverberate long after the leader has left. Cultures, precedents, and even unspoken norms can emerge from choices made in a single moment of power. This chapter explores the legacy effect of ownership, the way decisions continue to echo through time. It challenges the notion that responsibility ends with tenure and urges leaders to act not just for impact, but with foresight. It proposes tools to make choices today that will still reflect clarity, integrity, and courage a decade later.

12.1 Strategic Afterlives: Decisions That Shape Cultures for Decades

12.1.1

Some decisions die with the moment; they serve their purpose, fade away, and leave little trace. But then there are others, quiet, even seemingly routine choices, that echo long after the decision-maker has moved on. These are strategic afterlives. They shape the culture, influence behaviour, and become part of the organisation's identity.

Not because someone decreed it that way, but because people unknowingly carry them forward, generation after generation.

Think of a founder's insistence on transparency in all dealings. Or a wartime CEO's relentless push for efficiency and cost discipline.

Or a leader's silent tolerance of mediocrity under pressure. These choices, once responses to a specific context, can morph into norms, sometimes helpful, sometimes harmful. They shape hiring, decision-making speed, reward systems, and even the informal language of teams. Like inherited traits, they survive turnovers, restructurings, and rebranding exercises. They become how things are done here.

The paradox is this: leaders often underestimate how much permanence resides in their temporary decisions. A hiring policy created to address a short-term skill gap might unknowingly promote homogeneity for years. A rushed compromise made to meet a deadline might normalise cutting corners. Even unspoken signals, a leader who rewards only star performers but never team collaborators, can institutionalise competitiveness over cooperation.

Consider the famed story of Hewlett-Packard's 'HP Way'. What began as a set of informal leadership practices between Bill Hewlett and Dave Packard, management by walking around, respect for engineers, focus on innovation, evolved into a deeply rooted culture. It persisted even as the company grew globally, long after the founders had stepped back. The afterlife of their leadership decisions created an identity stronger than any strategy document.

(Extra Reading: https://www.jimcollins.com/article_topics/articles/the-hp-way.html)

The most profound strategic afterlives are those that aren't even noticed. They blend into the culture like background music, ever-present, but rarely questioned. That's where ownership gets tricky. Leaders may leave the building, but their thinking doesn't. It lingers in email etiquette, project prioritisation, feedback styles, and how people respond to failure.

And so, leadership isn't just about deciding well in the moment. It's about deciding in a way that stands the test of time, or at least understanding that you don't get to choose how long your choices live.

In every strategic decision, ask yourself: *What kind of ancestor am I being to this organisation?* Are you leaving behind legacies of empowerment or systems of dependence? Have you planted principles, or just preferences? Because whether you intended it or not, someone, years from now, will act in your name. And the question then will not be *what did you mean*, but *what did you leave behind?*

That's the echo of ownership.

12.1.2   A name that has stood for over a century: Tata

When Shri Jamsetji Tata laid the foundation of the Tata Group in the late 19th century, his decisions were far more than commercial. They were cultural. His conviction that business must serve society wasn't an afterthought; it was the centrepiece. At a time when industrialisation was synonymous with exploitation, he envisioned worker welfare schemes, housing colonies, and learning institutions, not as CSR, but as strategic necessity.

Fast forward to Shri JRD Tata, who carried the flame forward with a leadership style that combined sharp business acumen with human empathy. His commitment to ethical governance, fair employee treatment, and long-term value creation wasn't just personal; it became institutional. These decisions, grounded in values and vision, slowly calcified into the Tata Group's cultural DNA.

Decades later, when Shri Ratan Tata made the controversial call to exit businesses that didn't align with the Group's values - even at financial cost; it wasn't a fresh ethical awakening. It was a continuation. An echo of Jamsetji's and JRD's choices, still reverberating through the boardrooms and brand decisions.

Even newer entities under the Tata umbrella, like Tata Consultancy Services (TCS), inherited this cultural gravity. The company's cautious risk-taking, emphasis on client trust, and respect for employees didn't emerge in a vacuum. They are the ripple effects of old strategic decisions. Choices made long ago that continued to shape things long after their makers were gone.

On the other hand, consider the quieter consequences in other firms where short-term aggressiveness, leadership ego, or political convenience became templates. Many Indian conglomerates that once rode high on the waves of liberalisation struggled later, not because of market dynamics alone, but because their cultural foundations were shaped by strategic choices that glorified control over collaboration, speed over sustainability, and personal loyalty over professional merit. The afterlife of those decisions led to opaque governance, talent drain, and eventual decline.

The Indian corporate landscape is filled with examples, from thoughtfully built legacies to unintentional traps left behind. Here's the deeper truth. Leadership decisions are rarely neutral. They always sow something, whether it's trust or fear, openness or closed thinking, learning or complacency. And while strategies are rewritten every few years, cultures often follow older maps.

The question isn't just what are you deciding today? The more haunting one is: what culture will this decision be teaching, normalising, and institutionalising tomorrow?

The echoes don't ask for your permission.

12.1.3   The TCS Case: Integrity as a Cultural Echo

Strategic afterlives don't only emerge from grand declarations or company-wide initiatives. Sometimes, it's the way a team handles a single report, a single conversation, or a moment of truth that leaves behind the most enduring cultural imprint.

I had the opportunity to witness one such moment firsthand in the 1990s, when a Public Sector Undertaking (PSU) consulted Tata Consultancy Services (TCS) for guidance on a diversification strategy. The team working on the interim report, perhaps influenced by pressure to deliver quickly or by the client's strong internal views, incorporated suggestions that were more reflective of the PSU's own assumptions than an independent market assessment. On the surface, it may have seemed like a minor misstep. A draft, after all, can always be revised.

But what followed is where culture was quietly being written.

When TCS seniors discovered that the interim report lacked rigour and objectivity, they did not brush it aside as 'good enough' or push it through under client pressure. Instead, they became visibly upset, not out of image management, but from a deep-rooted belief in the sanctity of their professional responsibility. They offered a sincere apology to the PSU and insisted on going back to the drawing board. The final report was delivered only after a thorough, independent study of the market.

That decision, of owning the lapse, of refusing to compromise standards for convenience, might not have made headlines. But it made history within the organisation. It set a tone. It sent a message down the ranks: *We are not just a service provider; we are custodians of trust.* That one act of responsible leadership became a reference point for how TCS teams approach client work even today, with integrity, rigour, and intellectual honesty.

This is how cultural legacies are formed. Not through vision statements on websites, but in quiet conference rooms, in uncomfortable truths acknowledged, in standards upheld when no one is watching. The leaders involved in that moment might have moved on, but the cultural echo of that decision still shapes how the organisation behaves and is perceived.

It's a reminder that leadership decisions don't end with the decision-maker. They ripple forward through behaviour, reputation, and institutional conscience.

12.2   *Exit Paradoxes: Leaving Behind Control Without Leaving Behind Responsibility*

There comes a moment in every leader's journey when the stage must be yielded, the chair vacated, and the baton passed. It may come with a retirement, a promotion, a resignation, or sometimes, even with a forced exit. But here's the catch; while control may change hands, responsibility often does not.

This is the Exit Paradox.

We believe stepping down means letting go. But leadership, unlike a title or a badge, doesn't vanish when you walk out the door. You might no longer call the shots, but the echoes of your decisions, the culture you shaped, the systems you set in motion, the people you influenced, continue to ripple long after you're gone. And sometimes, you are held accountable for the consequences even when you're no longer in command.

12.2.1   The Ghosts of Choices Past

Every leader leaves behind a legacy, but not all legacies are intentional. Decisions that once seemed minor, a shortcut here, a compromise there, can evolve into systemic flaws or institutional habits. And when those repercussions surface, the world doesn't care whether you're still at the helm.

Responsibility, it turns out, has a longer shelf life than authority.

In organisations especially, successors often inherit not just responsibilities, but also the unresolved dilemmas, strategic miscalculations, or unaddressed cultural issues of those who came before. And while control is a baton passed cleanly in the relay, responsibility is more like a fragrance; it lingers, for better or worse.

12.2.2   Letting Go Without Abandoning

To exit well is to understand the subtle art of detachment without desertion. It means acknowledging that your influence persists, even in absence. That your name may still surface, in boardrooms, on battlefields of decisions, in whispered references during hard times.

True ownership, paradoxically, requires surrender.

You let go of micromanagement, but not of accountability. You let the new leaders find their path, but remain open to guide without imposing. You don't dictate outcomes, but you remain answerable, at least in conscience, for the seeds you once sowed.

The best leaders prepare for their exit long before it arrives, not just by grooming successors or handing over files, but by institutionalising values, embedding resilience, and encouraging independent thinking. They exit, not with erasure, but with continuity.

12.2.3   The Invisible Thread

This paradox is even more pronounced when the exit isn't your choice. Perhaps you're pushed out, overruled, or sidelined. Maybe you see the organisation taking a direction you never would've approved. The temptation is to distance yourself, wash your hands clean. But if you once shaped it, you're still part of its DNA.

You may no longer be its face, but you remain one of its architects.

And here's where the paradox deepens: the more meaningful your leadership was, the more impossible it is to walk away entirely. You don't just leave a position; you leave a presence. In the stories people tell. In the way meetings are run. In how challenges are approached.

That is both the burden and the blessing of true ownership; it never quite exits with you.

12.2.4   In the End, It's Not About Control

Control is momentary. Influence is enduring. And responsibility, at its purest, isn't tied to status or power, but to intention and consequence. As leaders, we must learn to navigate exits not as ends, but as transitions into new forms of stewardship.

Because even after we let go, we are still accountable, not to a role, but to the legacy we leave behind.

12.2.5   Reflection

Exiting a leadership role is often viewed as a clean break, but in reality, it rarely is. Leaders who have shaped people, systems, and decisions remain connected to outcomes whether or not they hold formal authority. Recognising this helps us plan exits more responsibly, not by trying to control what happens after us, but by being intentional about the structures, behaviours, and cultures we leave behind. Ownership doesn't end when control does, and the leaders who understand this are the ones who exit without abandoning the responsibilities they once claimed.

12.3   Designing Decisions with Future Ownership in Mind

12.3.1

Leaders often believe their job is to make decisions and move on. But the truth is, decisions are rarely confined to the moment; they echo forward. The best leaders understand this and act accordingly. They know that the choices they make today will become someone else's legacy to uphold, challenge, or repair tomorrow. This is why the ability to design decisions with future ownership in mind isn't just a strategic skill; it's an ethical one.

You're not just solving a problem; you're setting a precedent.

Every decision you make becomes part of a pattern. That policy you draft, that exception you allow, the person you promote, the compromise you accept; all of it will be seen, inherited, and interpreted by others. Sometimes, long after you've left the room, or the company, or even the world.

So, the question isn't *"What do I want now?"*

It's *"What will this mean to the person who inherits it later?"*

12.3.2   Legacy Through Design, Not Accident

When leaders are caught up in urgency, decisions often become transactional. *"Fix it now." "Get it done." "Let's move forward."* But if we pause just a moment longer and ask: *What does this enable or disable for the next leader?*, we shift from reactive leadership to regenerative leadership.

Decisions should be shaped with longevity, not just efficiency.

Will this decision require constant firefighting?

Will it empower or entrap those who follow?

Will it create clarity or confusion down the line?

These questions don't slow decision-making; they deepen it.

12.3.3   Designing for the Next Owner

Ownership doesn't end with your signature. It morphs, evolves, and finds new stewards. Designing with future ownership in mind means making choices that are:

Transparent – So others can understand why a decision was made.

Flexible – So successors can adapt without dismantling everything.

Values-Aligned – So even if the strategy shifts, the spirit endures.

Documented – So your reasoning isn't lost in oral tradition or forgotten context.

When your decisions are designed this way, you build institutional memory. And more importantly, you protect the integrity of those who come after you from having to guess, or worse, clean up, a poorly thought-through legacy.

12.3.4   The Unspoken Gratitude of the Future

You may never meet the person who inherits your decisions. But they'll feel your impact. They may thank you silently for your foresight, or curse your name for the burden. Either way, you will be present.

So think of every big decision like a letter to someone in the future: *"I was here. I cared. I tried to make this easier for you."*

Leadership isn't just about owning the moment.

It's about owning the ripple.

12.3.5   Anand Mahindra and the Architecture of Enduring Responsibility

Anand Mahindra didn't just inherit a business empire; he reimagined it for the future. When he took the reins of the Mahindra Group in the late 1990s, the company was largely known for tractors and utility vehicles. But rather than riding the momentum of legacy, Anand chose to redesign the company's identity around long-term relevance, responsible capitalism, and social impact.

One of his most future-facing decisions was embedding the philosophy of '*Rise*', not just as a marketing campaign, but as a guiding principle for the entire Group. '*Rise*' was designed as a shared vision to drive positive change and enable stakeholders, employees, customers, communities, to rise.

Crucially, this philosophy wasn't locked to his personality or presence. It was institutionalised into brand strategy, leadership training, sustainability metrics, and governance frameworks. Today, business leaders across sectors within the Mahindra Group, from finance to real estate to electric mobility, use '*Rise*' as a north star to align decisions, even as they face vastly different operational contexts.

Another important area where Anand Mahindra planned for future ownership is succession and decentralisation. He actively nurtured leadership pipelines and gave autonomy to business verticals, reducing dependence on a central figure. That's a mark of a leader thinking beyond ego, building for continuity, not control.

Even in public discourse, his social media presence and advocacy for ethical leadership, entrepreneurship, and inclusive growth have created a reputational platform that future Mahindra leaders inherit with both pride and responsibility.

By designing decisions that outlast his tenure, and his name, Anand Mahindra has shown that leadership is not about leaving your mark, but about lighting a path.

12.3.6   The Future Ownership Design Lens

When making leadership decisions, use this lens to ensure you're not just solving for now, but building for those who come after you.

1. Values: Embed Guiding Principles

Are your decisions anchored in timeless values?

Will those values remain relevant and respected after you're gone?

Example: 'Rise' as a moral compass at Mahindra Group, ensuring all verticals align with a higher purpose.

2. Structures: Institutionalise, Don't Personalise

Are the systems, policies, and governance mechanisms designed to function independently of you?

Will they empower successors without needing your presence or intervention?

Example: Decentralised leadership and clear succession pathways at Mahindra reduced dependency on Anand Mahindra as an individual.

3. Voices: Create Platforms That Speak Beyond You

Are you creating narratives, cultures, and platforms that allow others to continue the story?

Will future leaders have the language and license to interpret your vision with their own leadership voice?

Example: Anand Mahindra's public persona amplified ethical capitalism, but the ethos was carried forward by a broad base of leaders, not just one voice.

This framework encourages you to ask: "Will this decision remain wise when I'm no longer around to explain it?"

CHAPTER 13

The Ownership Mandal: Integrating the Paradoxes into Conscious Leadership

What if integrating paradox isn't a dilemma, but the very essence of mature leadership?

This chapter distils the paradoxes explored, from invisible decisions to emotional weight, inherited burdens to deferred blame, and weaves them into a coherent leadership philosophy. It invites the reader to build their own framework of inescapable ownership, not as a burden, but as a dynamic, generative force. Here, responsibility becomes not just something to manage, but something to embody with intention, courage, and clarity.

A *Mandal* (मण्डल) is a circular design that represents wholeness, balance, and unity. The word comes from Sanskrit, meaning 'circle', and it's often used in spiritual and meditative traditions to symbolise the universe, inner self, or life's journey.

Imagine a wheel with a central point and patterns radiating outward – everything is connected, everything has a place. A Mandal shows that many different parts can come together to form a complete, meaningful whole.

In the context of leadership and ownership:

The Ownership Mandal is a visual and mental model.

It brings together different paradoxes of leadership.

It helps leaders see how **Self, Others, Systems, and Legacy** are interconnected realms of responsibility.

Instead of viewing contradictions (like holding on vs. letting go) as conflicts, the Mandal helps us see them as complementary parts of a larger whole.

Why Use a Mandal?

It's not linear, just like leadership isn't.

It helps leaders navigate complexity by seeing patterns, not just problems.

It encourages *reflection, balance, and integration* – crucial qualities for conscious leadership.

13.1 Mapping the Paradoxes: From Contradictions to Completeness

Unifying the contradictions explored throughout the book into a coherent mental model of ownership.

By now, we've journeyed through the winding terrain of ownership, moving from the heavy weight of responsibility to the clarity and freedom it can offer. We've explored paradoxes that didn't seem to make sense at first. Like how avoiding ownership still makes you accountable. How taking on too much responsibility can harm just as much as not caring at all. And how staying emotionally distant can sometimes be the kindest way to lead. And in doing so, we've chipped away at the myth of simplicity, the notion that ownership is a single, straight-edged concept.

But now, we come to the point where we pause and look back, not just to admire the view, but to connect the dots.

This chapter is an invitation to move from fragmentation to wholeness. If earlier chapters held contradictions like two opposing poles of a magnet, now we attempt to see the magnetic field they together create. What emerges is not a formula but a Mandal, a layered, living model that holds these contradictions not as problems to be solved, but as patterns to be understood.

13.1.1   Accepting the Tensions, Not Resolving Them

Modern leadership often seeks comfort in binary thinking, right or wrong, strong or weak, leader or follower. But conscious leadership, especially when shaped by deep ownership, demands a higher tolerance for tension. The paradoxes we've discussed are not glitches in the system. They are features of what it means to lead consciously.

Consider this:

If ownership is inescapable, then pretending to avoid it only delays the reckoning.

If over-owning erodes others' agency, then sometimes stepping back is the most responsible act.

If emotional ownership drains the leader, then guarding one's inner space is not selfish; it is strategic.

These are not choices between two ends of a spectrum. They are dynamic balances we constantly calibrate. Conscious leadership means learning to hold both sides of the paradox without collapsing into either extreme.

13.1.2   A Mental Model, Not a Manual

The Ownership Mandal is not a checklist or a flowchart. It is a mental model; one that is best felt as much as understood. Picture it like a compass, not a GPS. It won't give you turn-by-turn directions, but it will help you orient yourself in complexity.

At the centre of it all is self-awareness. It is the calm place where you can see all the paradoxes clearly, without feeling anxious. Radiating outward are the core tensions:

Responsibility vs. Empowerment

Involvement vs. Detachment

Direction vs. Collaboration

Accountability vs. Humility

Vulnerability vs. Authority

Rather than seeing each of these as dilemmas to be 'fixed', we begin to view them as dual forces that create dynamic stability, much like the tension in a suspension bridge holds it up.

13.1.3   From Friction to Flow

As you internalise this model, something profound shifts. You no longer flinch when contradictions surface. You expect them. You even welcome them as signs that you're operating at a deeper, more nuanced level of leadership. This is where real mastery begins, not when you find all the answers, but when you learn how to live the questions well.

Owning outcomes, sharing credit, holding space, and setting direction; all begin to co-exist within you. There's less fragmentation, less guilt, and more flow. Your leadership ceases to be a series of reactive decisions. It becomes an integrated expression of presence, principle, and participation.

13.1.4   The Completion That Doesn't Close

This mapping is not an end. It's a synthesis that invites further unfolding. Like a Mandal, it reflects the inner order we bring to the outer chaos. It reminds us that completeness does not mean perfection;

it means coherence. The contradictions are still there. But now, they form a whole. And in that wholeness, we find the strange and beautiful truth. The more we understand the paradoxes of ownership, the more we become free to lead from wholeness, not as fractured parts, but as integrated beings.

13.1.5   Table: The Paradoxes of Ownership

Paradox	Tension Between	Insight
The Inescapable Accountability Paradox	Avoiding Responsibility vs. Being Held Responsible	Even refusal to act is a form of ownership through consequence.
The Over-Responsibility Trap	Taking Charge vs. Creating Dependency	Over-owning disempowers others and creates bottlenecks.
The Delegation Illusion	Delegating Authority vs. Abdicating Ownership	True delegation includes continued moral and emotional responsibility.
Emotional Ownership Dilemma	Compassion vs. Detachment	Caring deeply without burning out requires emotional boundaries.
Invisible Ownership	Silent Influence vs. Formal Authority	One can shape outcomes without overt control, and still be accountable.
Vulnerability–Authority Paradox	Showing Weakness vs. Earning Respect	Authenticity breeds trust, but must be balanced with responsibility.
Empowerment Paradox	Leading from the Front vs. Leading from Within	Empowering others involves letting go without losing alignment.
Systemic Ownership Conflict	Individual Agency vs. Organisational Culture	Ownership must align with systems, or it gets distorted and diluted.

Paradox	Tension Between	Insight
Accountability–Humility Paradox	Owning Success vs. Sharing Credit	True leaders attribute success outward and reflect failure inward.
Shared Ownership Paradox	Taking Responsibility vs. Distributing Ownership	Leadership maturity is knowing when to hold, share, or release ownership.

13.2 The Four Realms of Ownership: Self, Others, Systems, Legacy

A holistic framework for viewing leadership responsibility across personal, interpersonal, organisational, and intergenerational planes.

13.2.1

Leadership, in its truest form, is not confined to managing tasks or driving outcomes. It is the simple act of holding. Holding space for growth, for change, and for taking care of what matters. But what, exactly, do leaders hold? And for whom? These questions form the heart of ownership.

As we explore what it means to take inescapable ownership, we begin to see four deeply connected areas where it shows up most clearly; in how we lead ourselves, how we support others, how we shape systems, and how we leave behind a legacy.

Together, they form the Ownership Mandal, a symbolic integration of the internal and external, the immediate and the enduring, the visible and the subtle. Let us step into each realm, not as compartments, but as dimensions that breathe into one another.

1. Ownership of the Self: The Inner Ground of Leadership

All ownership begins with the self. This is not the ownership of ego or achievement, but the far deeper accountability of self-awareness, self-regulation, and self-alignment.

To lead others, one must first be willing to lead oneself, through confusion, through temptation, through the shadows we'd rather avoid. Emotional discipline, clarity of intent, the courage to confront one's own contradictions; these are not optional extras, they are the foundation.

When leaders bypass this inner work, their decisions are often driven by fear, insecurity, or the need for validation. But when self-ownership is firm, leadership becomes rooted and authentic. It doesn't seek power; it emanates presence.

Ownership of the self is where we ask:

Am I showing up with integrity, or am I hiding behind roles and titles?

2. Ownership of Others: The Interpersonal Ethic

The second realm extends outward; how we relate to people. Not as resources to be managed, but as individuals to be honoured.

Here, ownership is not control. It is responsibility without domination. It's the awareness that our words, our energy, our assumptions, especially as leaders, shape the psychological climate of those around us.

To own this realm is to own the ripple effects of our influence, to recognise when we empower, and when we diminish. To take responsibility for how we mentor, how we listen, how we include, and how we hold space for others to thrive.

This realm also brings a delicate paradox: we are responsible for people, but not instead of them. True leadership doesn't breed dependency; it cultivates ability to make your own choices and take responsibility for them.

Ownership of others invites us to ask:

Am I enabling growth, or fostering silent compliance?

3. Ownership of Systems: The Architecture of Culture

Leadership does not operate in a vacuum. Every decision is made within, and impacts, the systems we inhabit and shape. These systems may be formal (policies, processes, structures) or informal (norms, stories, power flows).

To lead with system ownership is to acknowledge that culture is not an accident. It's a reflection of what we permit, prioritise, and perpetuate.

Leaders who dodge this realm often fall into the trap of personal virtue, believing that being ethical or competent individually is enough. But unless we take responsibility for the environment we create, even the most well-intentioned leadership can unwittingly allow dysfunction to fester.

This is where structural change, inclusive design, and feedback loops become acts of ownership. Systems are slow to move, but they compound over time.

Ownership of systems dares us to ask:

What am I enabling through the culture I am choosing, silently or loudly, to uphold?

4. Ownership of Legacy: The Intergenerational Compass

The final realm lifts our gaze beyond the current quarter, the present project, or even our own tenure. It brings us into contact with the long arc of impact.

What are we leaving behind, not just in results, but in values? How will today's decisions echo tomorrow? Who inherits our choices? What stories will they tell?

This realm is perhaps the hardest to grasp, because it demands a patience and humility that modern leadership often resists. Legacy is not about statues or names on buildings; it's about the unseen seeds sown in the culture, the mindset, the pathways made easier for the next generation.

This kind of ownership is generative. It compels us to lead not for applause, but for alignment with something timeless. It's where stewardship overtakes short-termism.

Ownership of legacy whispers the question:

Am I building something that will outlast me in wisdom, not just in infrastructure?

13.2.2   The Mandal is Not a Sequence - It is a Circle

These four realms are not steps in a ladder. They are petals in a mandal, each informing and stabilising the others. If a leader owns the system but neglects the self, dissonance creeps in. If they own their interpersonal impact but ignore long-term legacy, vision becomes shortsighted.

Holistic ownership is dynamic. At times, one realm will call louder than the others. But sustainable, conscious leadership calls us to return again and again to the centre; where all four intersect.

13.2.3   Living the Ownership Mandal

To embody the Ownership Mandal is not to become perfect. It is to become present. To lead with an open heart and open eyes. To move from unconscious reaction to conscious integration.

And in doing so, leaders not only carry responsibility; they become responsibility. Not as a burden, but as a privilege.

13.2.4 Exemplars

1. Ownership of the Self: Ratan Tata's Inner Discipline and Restraint

Shri Ratan Tata is known for his calm demeanour, understated presence, and thoughtful leadership. But behind this exterior is a deep commitment to self-mastery. Despite leading one of India's largest conglomerates, he avoided flamboyance, resisted corporate arrogance, and held himself to the highest standards of personal integrity.

In 2008, when the Taj Mahal Palace Hotel in Mumbai was attacked by terrorists, Tata visited the site not for a photo opportunity, but to quietly meet every affected employee and their families. He ensured that no Taj employee was laid off and that every need, from medical care to compensation, was met without media fanfare.

He never used his position for self-aggrandisement. He fully embraced the emotional weight of the crises his people faced and led with a quiet sense of dignity. This was a result of deep self-awareness, humility, and ethical consistency.

Ownership of Self asks: *Am I showing up with integrity when no one is watching?*

2. Ownership of Others: Kiran Mazumdar-Shaw's Empathetic Leadership at Biocon

Ms. Kiran Mazumdar-Shaw, the founder of Biocon, is known not just for building a biotech empire, but for her deep sense of accountability toward people, including employees, patients, and society at large.

During the COVID-19 pandemic, she went beyond her company's call of duty. She provided testing kits at affordable prices, offered government partnerships, and ensured that Biocon employees were cared for, emotionally and physically.

Her leadership style is empathetic but empowering. She doesn't micromanage, but ensures her teams feel safe, respected, and heard. She once said, *"I think, in terms of corporate philosophy, I've always believed that you've got to treat people in a very, very egalitarian manner in the sense I like to treat people on a one to one basis. And I like people to take on a lot of responsibilities because I think with a sense of responsibility also comes a sense of purpose."*

Her sense of ownership for others extends into philanthropy, healthcare access, and inclusive hiring practices.

Ownership of Others asks: *Am I empowering people or overshadowing them?*

3. Ownership of Systems: E. Sreedharan and the Metro Model

When Shri E. Sreedharan took on the Delhi Metro project, he wasn't just building trains; he was redefining how infrastructure could be managed in India. Known as the "Metro Man of India," Sreedharan was committed to transparency, punctuality, and public accountability.

He didn't blame inefficiency on the 'system'. He became the system, by instituting clear processes, ethical procurement, and non-negotiable timelines. His leadership ensured that Phase 1 of the Delhi Metro was completed on time and within budget, a rarity in public sector projects.

He created a replicable system of governance and execution that proved that world-class infrastructure was possible in India without shortcuts or corruption.

Ownership of Systems asks: *Am I shaping the architecture that sustains excellence?*

4. Ownership of Legacy: Dr. A.P.J. Abdul Kalam's Quiet Contribution to India's Future

Dr. A.P.J. Abdul Kalam, India's 'Missile Man' and former President, lived and breathed legacy. He mentored countless young people, often taking time to meet students even after long days of work. He wrote books not just on science and strategy, but on values, dreams, and the purpose of life.

Though he contributed to India's defence capabilities, his greater gift was how he lit the spark of aspiration in millions. He lived modestly, spoke powerfully, and chose his actions through the lens of long-term national growth.

He often said, *"Dreams are not what you see in sleep; dreams are what don't let you sleep."* His legacy wasn't in the missiles he built; it was in the minds he inspired.

Lesson: *Legacy ownership is about planting trees under whose shade we may never sit.*

Summary

Realm	Leader	Illustrated Through	Key Takeaway
Self	Ratan Tata	Quiet dignity, moral clarity, emotional steadiness	Leadership begins with personal integrity
Others	Kiran Mazumdar-Shaw	Empathy during crises, people-first mindset	Empower others through care and trust
Systems	E. Sreedharan	Ethical execution in public projects	Systems can be a lever for national transformation
Legacy	Dr. A.P.J. Abdul Kalam	Mentorship, writing, shaping young minds	Think beyond tenure; create enduring value

13.3 *The Conscious Leadership Loop: Awareness, Action, Aftermath*

A cycle to help leaders navigate paradoxes with intentionality; what you perceive, what you choose, and what endures.

Leadership is not a straight path; it rarely ever has been. It is a looping journey, a dance between moments of insight, decisive movement, and the consequences that follow. At the heart of conscious leadership lies not a checklist of traits, but a living loop: **Awareness → Action → Aftermath**. This simple yet powerful cycle allows leaders to navigate paradoxes not just reactively, but intentionally. Let's step into each part of this loop.

13.3.1 Awareness: What You Perceive

Awareness is the pause before the move, the breath before the speech. It is where leadership truly begins.

Conscious leadership requires seeing clearly, not just what is happening, but why it is happening. It means paying attention to everything, including the external facts, the invisible undercurrents, and your own internal landscape of beliefs, biases, and triggers.

Are you reacting to pressure or responding to purpose? Are you seeing the problem, or the people entangled in it? Are you carrying old wounds into new decisions?

Without awareness, even the most well-meaning action can fall into unconscious patterns, command without empathy, courage without context, responsibility without reflection.

In this phase, leaders ask themselves:

What am I sensing, not just externally, but internally?

What assumptions am I making?

What paradoxes are showing up here?

This is not passive observation; it is an active, courageous honesty with oneself.

13.3.2   Action: What You Choose

Action is where awareness becomes embodied. It is the moment of choice.

This is not about perfection. It is about presence, choosing in alignment with your principles, not your pressures. It's where a leader risks clarity over popularity, alignment over appeasement, and meaning over mechanics.

Intentional action honours complexity. It acknowledges that sometimes there is no perfect answer, only the next honest step.

Leadership paradoxes often present themselves here in full force:

Should I step in or step back?

Do I protect the team or push their boundaries?

Do I take full control or invite co-ownership?

Conscious action is not about avoiding these tensions; it's about leaning into them with integrity. It is where strategy meets soul.

In this phase, ask:

Am I choosing from fear or from alignment?

Does this action serve the greater good or merely my own comfort?

What values are guiding this decision?

13.3.3   Aftermath: What Endures

Every action leaves a footprint. This is where leadership's long game is played.

The aftermath is not just the result; it is the ripple. It reveals what our choices truly meant. Often, it is only in hindsight that the wisdom, or the cost, of our actions becomes visible.

But this isn't just about evaluation. It's about evolution.

Leaders who revisit the aftermath with humility, not blame, grow deeper roots. They reflect not just on outcomes, but on how those outcomes align with their intention. They don't just ask, *"Did it work?"* They ask, *"What did I learn, and what did I leave behind?"*

Ownership doesn't end with action; it extends into this reflective space. The impact we have may live on in others long after our role is done.

In this phase, ask:

What was the true impact of my action, on people, culture, purpose?

Did I stay true to my awareness, or get swept up in the moment?

What story does this aftermath now tell?

13.3.4   Closing the Loop, And Beginning Again

The Conscious Leadership Loop is not linear. It is not a project to finish. It is a practice to inhabit. The leader who returns to this loop becomes more than a problem-solver; they become a mirror, a compass, and sometimes, a quiet revolution.

When leaders commit to awareness before action, and reflection after, they begin to lead not just from the head, but from wholeness. They stop treating paradoxes as burdens and start seeing them as invitations, to evolve, to deepen, and to lead with presence.

And so, the loop continues: *what you perceive, what you choose, and what endures.*

13.4   *Holding and Releasing: The Art of Responsible Detachment*

When to embrace ownership fully – and when leadership means letting go without abdication.

Leadership, at its core, is an act of deep engagement. You step forward. You take charge. You assume responsibility for outcomes - seen and unseen, expected and emergent. But what happens when the very act of holding on too tightly begins to choke initiative, dim creativity, and create silent dependency?

This is where the paradox lives: in knowing when to take the reins, and when to let them slip through your fingers with intention.

13.4.1   The Illusion of Control

One of leadership's most enduring delusions is the idea that holding on equals responsibility. We equate control with commitment, micromanagement with care, oversight with diligence. But real leadership matures when we realise that control is not synonymous with stewardship. Sometimes, the most powerful form of ownership is the willingness to release.

To let go doesn't mean you stop caring. It means you choose to care differently.

It means trusting the seed you planted, even if the harvest is no longer yours to reap. It means letting others stumble, knowing the bruise might teach more than your intervention ever could. And it means stepping back without stepping away, present, available, but not invasive.

13.4.2   The Two Hands of Leadership

Picture leadership as holding life in two hands.

One hand is the hand of holding. It is strong, decisive, grounded. This hand takes charge, makes the tough call, absorbs the heat. It carries the weight of vision, direction, accountability.

The other is the hand of releasing. It is open, graceful, wise. This hand lets go of ego, control, and the need to be central. It creates space for others to rise. It detaches, not from responsibility, but from the illusion that all outcomes depend solely on you.

True leadership learns to use both hands. Knowing when to clench and when to open. When to stand firm and when to bow out. When to speak, and when to stay silent.

13.4.3   Responsible Detachment: Not Abdication, But Elevation

There's a difference between abdication and responsible detachment.

Abdication is dropping the ball. It's walking away when things get hard, refusing accountability, or blaming others.

Responsible detachment is staying anchored in values, purpose, and clarity, while consciously choosing not to interfere, manipulate, or micromanage. It's allowing others to own the process, even when their choices diverge from your instincts.

This is leadership not as domination, but as elevation.

You guide the arc without scripting every word. You trust the current while still scanning the horizon. You release your grip, not your grounding.

13.4.4   A Story from the Edge

A real-life story that comes from a high-pressure or critical situation, often where decisions are tough and outcomes are uncertain. It shows how leadership is tested at the boundaries, not in comfort zones.

A shipbuilder once told me how his most liberating moment as a project head came not from solving a technical crisis, but from not solving it.

A young engineer had made a poor design judgment. The instinct was to step in, fix it, and save time. But instead, the leader waited. He let the engineer wrestle with the consequences, supported quietly but without interference. The young man corrected his mistake, better than the leader could have, and walked away with a confidence that no lecture could have given him.

The leader later said, *"I realised my job wasn't to protect him from failure. My job was to hold the space where he could rise."*

That is the art of responsible detachment.

The Mandal Moment

Within the Ownership Mandal, this paradox is vital. We are not asked to abandon ownership, but to refine it, to hold it with humility and to release it with wisdom. Ownership is not always visible. Sometimes, the deepest ownership is invisible, like the hand that steadies a ladder but never climbs it.

To lead is to love without possession. To release without disconnecting. To carry responsibility not like a burden but like a gift, and to know when the gift must be passed on.

That is the quiet strength of conscious leadership.

That is the paradox of holding, and letting go.

13.5   Rituals of Integration: Daily Practices for Embodied Ownership

Translating Insight into Habit – Practical, Repeatable Behaviours that Reinforce Grounded Leadership

13.5.1

In leadership, insight without implementation has limited value. Awareness must translate into sustained behaviour. Ownership, as we've explored throughout this book, is not a conceptual exercise; it is a practice. To embody ownership consistently, leaders must internalise it through structured, repeatable habits that align mindset with action.

The following practices are designed to help leaders move from understanding to integration, creating a cadence of self-alignment, accountability, and cultural reinforcement. These are not time-intensive processes but purposeful rituals that anchor leadership behaviour in clarity and consistency.

1. Morning Alignment (Daily – 5 to 10 minutes): Start the day with intention. Before engaging with the operational tempo, take a few minutes to reflect:

What are the key responsibilities I need to own today?

What behaviours will best reflect my leadership values?

This helps leaders shift from reactive execution to deliberate response.

2. Midday Reset (Daily – 2 to 5 minutes): In the midst of meetings and deliverables, insert a brief pause. Step away, close the laptop, or sit silently for a moment. Ask:

Am I operating from clarity or reactivity?

Am I enabling ownership in others or centralising control?

This recalibration often prevents misalignment before it escalates.

3. Evening Review (Daily – 5 minutes): A short journal or digital note at the end of each day:

Where did I demonstrate ownership in a way that created clarity or impact?

Where did I default to blame, avoidance, or overreach?

Documenting these patterns builds reflective leadership and fosters internal accountability over time.

4. Team Ownership Huddle (Weekly – 30 minutes): Once a week, replace a transactional update meeting with a focused conversation on team dynamics and shared responsibility. Suggested prompts:

What went well and why?

What barriers are we encountering, and what can we each own differently?

What's one thing each member commits to improving or taking charge of?

This simple rhythm builds psychological safety and nurtures a culture of distributed ownership.

5. Delegation Audit (Weekly or Biweekly – 15 minutes): Review current priorities and responsibilities. Ask:

What am I holding that could be better executed by someone else?

What opportunities am I missing to build team capability?

This ritual prevents burnout and reinforces the distinction between ownership and micromanagement.

6. Boundary Review (Weekly – 10 minutes): Leadership sustainability requires maintaining boundaries. Once a week, reflect on:

Where did I say "yes" when I should have said "no"?

What boundary must I re-establish to protect focus and integrity?

This ensures leaders operate from clarity, not compromise.

7. Leadership Self-Review (Monthly – 30 minutes): Once a month, schedule time to step back and assess your leadership effectiveness beyond operational metrics:

Would I follow myself based on the last 30 days of decisions and behaviours?

What feedback am I avoiding, and what insight might it offer?

What habits need reinforcement or recalibration?

This structured review prevents drift and ensures the alignment of behaviour with purpose.

13.5.2   Embodied Ownership is Built, Not Assumed

Leadership does not mature through occasional brilliance but through disciplined consistency. These rituals are not meant to complicate already demanding schedules; they are strategic investments in clarity, culture, and character.

By integrating these practices into the rhythm of leadership, insight becomes habit. Ownership shifts from being a reactive burden to a proactive mindset. And over time, leaders not only drive results but shape cultures grounded in responsibility, trust, and long-term performance.

13.5.3   Further Reading

For Deeper Insight into the Practices of Embodied and Conscious Leadership

The following authors and books offer frameworks and insights that align with the rituals and behaviours described in this chapter. While

The Paradox of Inescapable Ownership presents an original synthesis, these works provide valuable context, tools, and inspiration for leaders committed to integrating ownership into daily practice:

Peter M. Senge – The Fifth Discipline: Introduces the idea of the learning organisation and stresses the importance of personal mastery, systems thinking, and reflective practice in leadership.

Stephen R. Covey – The 7 Habits of Highly Effective People: Emphasises aligning behaviour with principles and building proactive, value-driven routines. Covey's focus on intentionality, clarity, and discipline directly supports the formation of leadership rituals.

James Clear – Atomic Habits: Offers a powerful framework for creating lasting change through small, consistent habits. His idea of 'identity-based habits' aligns with the transition from insight to daily ownership.

Robert Kegan and Lisa Lahey – Immunity to Change: Explores the internal barriers that resist behavioural transformation and the structured practices needed to overcome them, valuable for understanding leadership inertia.

Bill George – True North: Explores authentic leadership grounded in self-awareness, purpose, and integrity. His emphasis on reflection and aligned action resonates with daily rituals of conscious leadership.

Patrick Lencioni – The Five Dysfunctions of a Team: Focuses on trust, accountability, and collective ownership, relevant to weekly team practices that build culture and reinforce responsibility.

Brene Brown – Dare to Lead: Introduces vulnerability, boundary-setting, and clarity of values as essential leadership behaviours. Her emphasis on emotional courage supports the human depth behind ownership.

Marshall Goldsmith – Triggers Creating Behaviour That Lasts: Provides practical tools for self-monitoring and leadership behaviour change through daily reflection questions, a direct inspiration for evening reviews and self-accountability routines.

13.6   *The Mandal Within: Designing Your Own Code of Responsible Leadership*

As we come to the end of this chapter, it's time to pause and turn inward.

You've explored different sides of leadership, the paradoxes, the purpose behind it, and the importance of being fully present. Now, the next step is to bring it all together in a way that feels personal and real to you.

Let's call this your leadership mandal. A mandal is a symbol, a circle that represents wholeness, balance, and unity. In the same way, your leadership mandal can be a space where all your thoughts, experiences, and lessons come together. Even the opposites, like strength and softness, action and patience, can sit side by side here, not as conflicts, but as parts of the whole.

So take a moment to reflect:

What are the biggest lessons you've learned about responsibility and leadership?

What kind of leader do you truly want to be, not for others, but for yourself?

What values guide you when no one is watching?

Now, imagine creating your own simple code of leadership. This could be a few short lines that capture how you want to show up as a leader every day.

Here's one example:

"I will lead with honesty and care. I will take responsibility when needed, and allow others to grow by letting go. I will listen deeply, act wisely, and always remember why I lead."

Your version might look different; and that's the point. It should feel true to you.

If it helps, draw a circle on a piece of paper. Write your core value or purpose in the centre. Around the circle, place a few qualities or paradoxes you want to embrace, like 'firm and kind,' 'focused and flexible,' or 'confident and curious.'

This is your leadership mandal, a quiet reminder of who you are when you lead from the inside out.

You don't have to be perfect. You just have to be present. And committed to growing, step by step, in your own way.

So as you move forward, carry this mandal within you. Let it guide your choices, calm your doubts, and remind you of the leader you are becoming.

This is your path. This is your promise.

CHAPTER 14

Case Study

The Legacy Engine – One Organisation, All the Paradoxes

How Generations of Toyota Leaders Navigated the Paradoxes of Ownership

"My name is on every car." - Akio Toyoda

Related: Chapter 12.1: The Ownership Echo

In a corporate world often intoxicated by disruption and individual charisma, Toyota offers a different narrative. It's the one of continuity, quiet responsibility, and an intergenerational commitment to improvement that speaks louder than any keynote speech. Toyota didn't just build vehicles. It built a system of ownership that transcended generations, embedded not in job descriptions but in culture, conscience, and character.

Toyota is not a hero story. It's a relay. And at every leg of the journey, someone chose to carry forward the baton, not because they were forced to, but because they understood a deeper truth: *You are responsible for more than what you control.*

This final chapter brings the entire paradox of inescapable ownership to life.

Recommended Video: https://www.facebook.com/watch/?v=1011281 230540594&rdid=PeU6e5pmrQRUDcKN

14.1   *Inheriting Ghosts You Didn't Create*

Related: Chapter 10 – Inherited Responsibility

When Kiichiro Toyoda took a decisive risk in the 1930s to start Toyota's automotive division, he did not do so from a blank slate. He inherited his father Sakichi's legacy, one rooted in innovation and frugality through loom manufacturing, and he felt responsible for transforming that legacy into something greater.

But Kiichiro didn't just inherit a family name. He inherited expectation. Pressure. Risk. He bet the company on an automobile vision when Japan had no automotive ecosystem. The tools didn't exist. The funding barely held. And the war loomed. Yet, he took the risk.

But when Toyota neared bankruptcy in 1950, he was blamed for the losses, despite having created the very vision that would ultimately lead Toyota to global prominence. Kiichiro resigned in shame.

His resignation was a silent echo of *Chapter 9: The Cost of Not Being Blamed.* In stepping down, he wasn't escaping responsibility; he was absorbing it, shielding the company so it could survive.

Leadership sometimes means falling for what others may one day rise from.

14.2   *Sacrificial Ownership: Not All Recognition is Immediate*

Related: Chapter 1.1, Chapter 5.3

Takeshi Ishida, Kiichiro's successor, had to lead through the ashes of that difficult moment. His role was not to innovate but to stabilise, rebuild trust, and continue a project he did not start. *Ishida's leadership exemplifies the inescapable ownership paradox:* Even if you don't make the original decision, once it reaches your desk, it becomes yours.

He didn't build the engine, but he chose to carry it forward.

Leadership, as we've explored, is not only about accepting the glory of impact, but carrying the unseen weight of someone else's unfinished task *(Chapter 10.1)*. Ishida chose to be responsible for a legacy that wasn't his, and because of that, Toyota lived.

14.3   Culture as a Carrier of Ownership

Related: Chapter 13.2 – The Four Realms of Ownership (Self, Others, Systems, Legacy)

It was under Eiji Toyoda and Taiichi Ohno that Toyota truly codified ownership, not as a top-down directive, but as a culture lived by every worker, engineer, and line manager.

The Toyota Production System (TPS) did not just revolutionise manufacturing. It created an ecosystem of distributed ownership *(Chapter 6.3)*, where the power to stop the line wasn't limited to the top. It belonged to the people closest to the problem.

"Any worker can pull the cord." - A TPS Principle

This wasn't delegation. It was trust. It was ownership without proximity to power.

You didn't need a title to be accountable.

Toyota's system manifested responsibility by design, with built-in feedback loops that made every invisible decision visible *(Chapter 2.3)* before it could become a crisis.

The cultural paradox? The more ownership was spread, the clearer it became.

14.4   *When Delegation Doesn't Abdicate Responsibility*

Related: Chapter 7 – Ownership by Proxy

Toyota succeeded, not because it had flawless decision-makers; it succeeded because it created mechanisms where delegation carried clarity, not moral detachment.

When Toyota opened manufacturing plants in the U.S., many predicted failure. How could a Japanese culture of precision and harmony survive in a different labour ethos? But Toyota succeeded, not by imposing control, but by transferring values, rituals, and responsibility.

Leaders at Toyota understood what we explored in *Chapter 7*: delegation is not relief; it is replication of responsibility with integrity.

14.5   *The Guilt Gap, The Echo, and The Renewal*

Related: Chapter 8.1, Chapter 12.1

Fast-forward to the 2009–2010 global recall crisis. Akio Toyoda, then President and grandson of Kiichiro, was summoned before the U.S. Congress to answer for unintended acceleration defects.

He could have distanced himself. The faults weren't entirely under his watch. The crisis was global. The data was inconclusive. But Akio did what only a true leader can:

He owned it anyway. *"I am deeply sorry for any accident that Toyota drivers have experienced."* - Akio Toyoda, Congressional Testimony

In that moment, Akio became the embodiment of emotional ownership (*Chapter 8*). The vehicles may not have failed because of his direct decisions, but the weight was his to bear. He didn't feel guilty because he was legally responsible; he felt responsible because he morally belonged to the outcome.

The legacy of ownership had come full circle. His grandfather resigned in silence to save the company. Akio stood in public and protected its soul.

And in that moment, Toyota began its renewal.

14.6   *Ritualising Ownership, Not Just Systematising It*

Related: Chapter 13.5 – Rituals of Integration

Toyota's journey is not a template; it is a testimony.

To how ownership is not just taught, but lived.

Not just in crisis, but in daily discipline.

Not in the corner office, but on the factory floor.

Not once, but over and over, across generations.

Toyota didn't just teach us about manufacturing.

It taught us about legacy.

About humility.

And most importantly, about how leadership decisions outlive you (*Chapter 12*).

14.7   *Closing the Loop – The Mandal in Motion*

Related: Chapter 13.1–13.6

You've journeyed through paradoxes that frustrate clarity and defy simple rules.

You've explored the weight of knowledge, the trap of savior-hood, and the illusions of shared blame.

And now, with Toyota as a mirror, you see how all of these can be held, harmonised, and passed on.

Toyota is not perfect. But it refused to be casual about what it carried.

That is what this book ultimately invites you to do:

To carry, to choose, and to pass on, not just tasks, but truths.

Ownership is not a burden. It is a bond, between what was, what is, and what could be.

And now, with every chapter behind you, the real work begins:

What will you own that no one asked you to?

What will you hold, even when no one else sees?

And what legacy will your leadership echo into time?

Note on Sources and Attribution

The concepts, frameworks, and reflections presented in this book are original in expression but draw upon a broad base of philosophical, managerial, and spiritual literature accumulated over centuries. Many of the underlying influences, particularly on ethics, leadership, and responsibility, have been referenced in detail in my prior publication, *The Ethical Strategist – Crafting Success through Values-Driven Leadership*. Readers are referred to that volume for a comprehensive list of sources and acknowledgements.

This work builds upon those foundations, extending the ideas into new contexts and interpretations. All efforts have been made to ensure proper attribution through that documented source.

About the Author

Deepak Rajaninath Mokashi is a distinguished professional with over four decades of experience in the fields of engineering, shipbuilding, corporate management, and strategic planning.

An accomplished Chartered Engineer and Fellow of the Institution of Engineers, the Institution of Marine Engineers, and the Institution of Valuers, Mokashi's technical expertise includes shipbuilding, project planning, ERP, and quality control.

His notable contributions in corporate management include the optimisation of production schedules, drafting MDL's corporate plan, and pioneering strategic initiatives that have shaped the organisation's current success. Mokashi's deep understanding of organisational transformation and risk management is underscored by his role as Technical Advisor to the Chairman & Managing Director of Mazagon Dock Shipbuilders Limited (MDL).

Beyond his corporate career, Mokashi has made significant contributions to national defence, including serving as a member co-opted by the Ministry of Defence for negotiation of India's first indigenous aircraft carrier project.

He has contributed to knowledge-sharing initiatives driving technological advancement and innovation as Member Secretary of the prestigious 'Society of Defence Technologists' that represents leading Indian defence organisations.

In addition to his technical prowess, Mokashi has also served for over three years as First Secretary at the Embassy of India in Moscow, representing India's diplomatic interests and delivering national projects.

His contributions extend to the arbitration field, where he served as the single technical expert for a high-stakes case between ONGC and Reliance Naval.

Mokashi has also authored various technical papers.

As an author of five published books, Mokashi brings a unique blend of corporate strategy, leadership, and philosophy, with a particular focus on ethics, resilience, and the Bhagawad Geeta's application to modern-day challenges.